PROJECT BASED LEARNING FOR THE AUSTRALIAN CURRICULUM

WHY DO WE TELL STORIES?

AND OTHER EPIC ENGLISH PROJECTS FOR YEARS 7–8

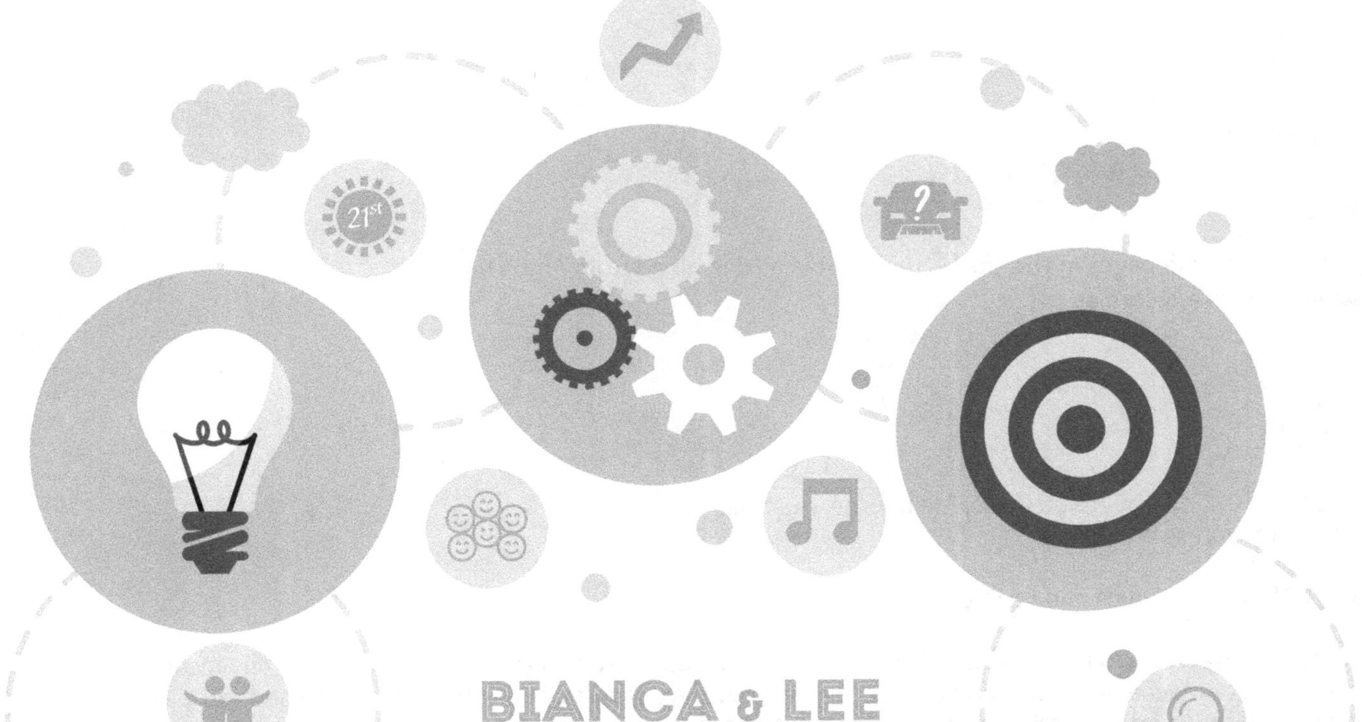

BIANCA & LEE HEWES

amba press

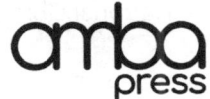

The reproducible pages in this book are available to download from Amba Press
www.ambapress.com.au

Published in 2025 by Amba Press, Melbourne, Australia
www.ambapress.com.au

© 2025 Bianca Hewes and Lee Hewes

All rights reserved. No part of this book may be reproduced or transmitted in any form or by any means, electronic or mechanical, including photocopying, recording or by any information storage and retrieval system, without prior permission in writing from the publisher.

Previously published in 2016 by Hawker Brownlow Education.
This edition replaces all previous editions.

ISBN: 9781923403000 (pbk)
ISBN: 9781923403017 (ebk)

A catalogue record for this book is available from the National Library of Australia.

CONTENTS

How to Use This Book

Part One: The What, Why and How of Project Based Learning   1

    What is Project Based Learning (PBL)?   1
    Why English Teachers Should Care About PBL   2
    How Does PBL Run in the English Classroom   4
    Project Outline   5
    Need to Know   5
    Expert/Rockstar   7
    Hook Lessons   7
    Project Walls   8
    PBL at a Glance   10
    Practice Projects   12
    Project Based Learning and the General Capabilities   12
    A Word About PBL and Assessment   19

Part Two: Sample Projects   21

Year 7 projects:

1. Game 2 Learn   23
   - Driving Question: Should video games be used to help us learn in secondary school?
   - Type of Text: Persuasive (speech)

2. #LOVEOZYA   37
   - Driving Question: How might reading Australian young adult fiction help teens make positive life decisions?
   - Type of Text: Imaginative (novel), informative/persuasive/imaginative (multimodal text)

3. Sustainable News   57
   - Driving Question: How can we, as citizen journalists, inform our local community about the importance of sustainable living?
   - Type of Text: Informative (news reports)

4. Reading Reimagined   67
   - Driving Question: How can technology be harnessed to enhance the reading experiences of teens?
   - Type of Text: Persuasive (pitch)

5. Acting Up! — 79
   - Driving Question: Why do we tell stories?
   - Type of Text: Imaginative (play script)

Year 8 projects:

1. Bodacious Balladeers — 87
   - Driving Question: How can we, as balladeers, tell the tales of our town?
   - Type of Text: Imaginative (ballad) and informative (report – optional)

2. Awesome Auteurs — 101
   - Driving Question: How can we pay homage to our favourite auteurs through a three-minute film?
   - Type of Text: Informative (feature article) and imaginative (short film)

3. Life Stories — 115
   - Driving Question: Whose moment of change will I preserve in the amber of narrative?
   - Type of Text: Imaginative (short story)

4. Soule of the Age — 125
   - Driving Question: Why do we continue to value the life and works of William Shakespeare?
   - Type of Text: Persuasive (display for festival) and imaginative (plays/sonnets)

5. Steampunk Stories — 135
   - Driving Question: What does the future hold for humanity?
   - Type of Text: Informative, imaginative and persuasive

Part Three: Additional Resources — 143

Acknowledgements — 160
Image Credits — 160

HOW TO USE THIS BOOK

Why Do We Tell Stories? And Other Epic English Projects for Years 7–8 is the second book in the Project Based Learning for the Australian Curriculum series. The first book, also written for English teachers, is called *Are Humans Wild at Heart? And Other Epic English Projects for Years 9–10* (Hawker Brownlow Education, 2016).

This book has been designed to support you as you begin experimenting with Project Based Learning (PBL) in your English classroom. Of course, the methodology of PBL is relevant to areas other than English — it can be used in a range of subjects, with many projects actually integrating more than one subject across the curriculum. Trying out something new in the classroom is always a daunting experience because feedback on success or failure is immediate. But the great thing about PBL is that it is creative for both the teacher and the student, and that means that experimentation, and sometimes failure, is a natural part of the process. Of course, no-one likes to feel like a failure, so we've structured this book into three distinct parts, designed to help you feel supported in your PBL journey.

PART ONE: THE WHAT, WHY AND HOW OF PROJECT BASED LEARNING

The first part of the book provides you with some background information about the nature and purpose of PBL, as well as outlining key strategies to ensure a successful and enjoyable learning experience for you and your students. This section also includes a discussion of how assessment works in PBL, as well as the relationship between PBL and the Australian Curriculum's General Capabilities.

PART TWO: SAMPLE PROJECTS

The second part of the book provides you with a selection of sample projects suitable for students in Years 7 and 8. You will be pleasantly surprised to find that a lot of the activities in this section look familiar — that's because PBL is about taking the best teaching strategies and repurposing them. The difference with PBL is that it empowers students to see a purpose for their learning beyond the classroom and to feel confident that they know where they are headed as they move through the project process.

Each project includes the following:

- [ ] Driving question
- [ ] Project outline
- [ ] Summary of learning experiences
- [ ] Literacy focus
- [ ] Specific mode(s) and text form(s)
- [ ] 21st-century skills
- [ ] Assessment strategies
- [ ] A range of resources to support learning

For both Years 7 and 8, there are two very detailed projects. We have given you a week-by-week outline of how the projects can be run with your students, as well as providing useful resources to support implementation of your first projects. Once you have implemented a couple of projects, and you begin to feel more confident with PBL, the remaining projects will act as loose guides. These projects are much less detailed, allowing you more scope to adapt and develop them to suit your students' needs and interests.

NOTE: It is essential that you adapt the given projects to make them meet the needs and interests of your students. Central to effective PBL is student ownership of learning and this can only be achieved if they feel that the project is relevant to their experiences and context. What may be considered significant and relevant to students on Sydney's Northern Beaches may have no relevance to students from Broome, Western Australia.

PART THREE: ADDITIONAL RESOURCES

The third part of the book is full of extra resources to help you design and run your own engaging projects for your English classes.

NOTE: Throughout this book you will see the icons below. These will help you to navigate the projects and easily identify the key content and elements of each project.

ONLINE RESOURCES

Each reproducible page within *Why Do We Tell Stories? And Other Epic English Projects for Years 7–8* is also available to download in .pdf file format from Amba Press www.ambapress.com.au.

PART ONE
THE WHAT, WHY AND HOW OF PROJECT BASED LEARNING

WHAT IS PROJECT BASED LEARNING (PBL)?

Project Based Learning is an inquiry-driven methodology that engages students in relevant, real-world problems that require them to attain and strengthen skills essential for success in the 21st century – collaboration, communication, creativity and digital citizenship.

The highly successful Project Based Learning approach outlined in our book has been developed over the last several years in the context of Australian primary and secondary schools. This is not to say, however, that the approach would not be useful in any other context. Our PBL approach is characterised by three interconnected learning stages: Discover, Create and Share. This process sees teachers and students inquire into a particular topic (Discover) and create a product (Create) to be shared with an authentic audience (Share). We feel that this structure gives students support as they move through a project and that the overarching approach authentically reflects the design and composition process undertaken by individuals working in creative fields relevant to the study of English. Creating products for an outside audience necessitates that students solve problems that have implications for the world outside of the classroom. Students need to consider to whom they are pitching their product or ideas, in which medium and how to best reach that audience in order to design something that will be of value to them.

During Project Based Learning, students may work individually or in a small team, depending on the nature of the project. The ideal team size is four students, as this allows every student to have an opportunity to contribute meaningfully to project work. The duration of a project will vary, depending on the nature of the inquiry and the composition. We have found that shorter projects are effective when you are first introducing PBL to your students. The projects in this book range from four weeks to six weeks in length. If a project is too long, you risk students becoming disengaged. We have also included a couple of single-lesson practice projects on pages 145–146 and information on this process can be found on 12.

The role of the teacher is different in a PBL classroom to that of a teacher in an exclusively teacher-centred classroom. Your role will change throughout the different stages of the project. For the majority of the time you will be there to support student learning by working closely with students individually or in small groups. There will be times where you will teach in a more traditional teacher-centred style, especially when you're introducing project requirements or instructing the whole-class on important content or skills. As a PBL teacher you must be very flexible, and keep a close eye on students' learning to ensure that you can support their needs "just in time".

It's important at this early stage to point out that PBL is not the same as "doing a project". Traditionally, school projects come at the *end* of a unit of work in the form of some type of artefact that students must create — at home, and often with the assistance of their parents — to demonstrate what they have learned. Obvious examples of these are cardboard posters about Shakespeare's life, a clay pyramid, a model of the Solar System or an "ancient" parchment made with old tea bags. These objects are submitted to the teacher with the purpose of being assessed. With PBL the project does not come at the end of learning, it *is* the learning. The focus is on how students discover content and develop skills through the process of inquiry, in class and with the full support of their teacher, in order to create something or present something to a public audience.

PBL typically contains several fundamental components, outlined in the **HOW DOES PBL RUN IN THE ENGLISH CLASSROOM?** section, with detailed examples given throughout the course of the book.

WHY ENGLISH TEACHERS SHOULD CARE ABOUT PBL: INTEGRATING MULTILITERACIES, FORMATIVE ASSESSMENT AND DIGITAL TECHNOLOGIES

There is impetus for pedagogical change in the English classroom. This impetus stems from our rapidly changing world, as observed by Bull and Anstey (2010, p. 6): "literacy teaching and learning should respond to the rapid changes in literacy arising from increasing globalization, technology and social diversity." This transforming social, cultural and technological landscape influences the responsibilities of the secondary English teacher in Australia and brings with it a set of new challenges. Three of these challenges are the purposeful integration of digital technologies into the classroom, the nature of assessment and the necessity to teach multiliteracies. It can be argued that these challenges may be successfully overcome by the reshaping of traditional teacher-centred pedagogy in the Australian secondary English classroom to a more student-centred and inquiry-based pedagogy. In fact, this impetus towards pedagogical change is reflected in the new Australian Curriculum: English.

Over the last ten years, English teachers have increasingly faced the challenge of when, how and why to introduce digital technologies into their lessons. Moreover, the Australian Curriculum: English stipulates that teachers are required to help students to become productive, creative and confident users of technology. The types of digital technologies that are beginning to be seen in educational settings include a combination of fixed (televisions, Interactive Whiteboards [IWBs], computer lab) and mobile technologies (iPads, iPods, mobile phones) as well as the software and web-based tools teachers and students access. Digital technologies that teachers and students bring into the English classroom should be meaningfully integrated into learning activities.

A second challenge faced by secondary English teachers in Australia is the nature of assessment. Often, the primary assessment in English is summative, despite evidence that formative or assessment for learning practices have "more impact on learning than any other general factor" (Petty, 2006). The Australian Curriculum: English advocates assessment for learning practices, including peer and self-assessment. In their seminal paper, "Inside the black box: Raising standards through classroom assessment", Black and Wiliam (1998) conclude that the introduction of effective assessment for learning "will require significant changes in classroom practice" (p. 141), because "instruction and formative assessment are indivisible" (p. 143). Importantly, Black and Wiliam propose that "what is needed is a classroom culture of questioning and deep thinking, in which pupils learn from d discussions with teachers and peers" (p. 146). These features are key elements of project-based pedagogies which have been shown to "have documented positive changes for teachers and students in motivation, attitude toward learning, and skills, including work habits, critical thinking skills and problem-solving" (Barron and Darling-Hammond, p. 4, 2008).

The final challenge facing English teachers today is the necessity to teach multiliteracies. The term "multiliteracies" was coined by the New London Group (Cazden, et al., 1996) and is defined as "a new approach to literacy teaching [that] overcomes the limitations of traditional approaches by emphasizing how negotiating the multiple linguistic and cultural differences in our society is central to the pragmatics of the working, civic, and private lives of students". A three-year ethnographic study by Mizuko et al (2008) describes how "new media allow for a degree of freedom and autonomy for youth that is less apparent in a classroom setting" (p. 2) and concludes that "the diversity in forms of literacy (accessed by young people) means it is problematic to develop a standardised set of benchmarks to measure" (p. 2) multiliteracies. Traditionally English in Australia has been viewed as a teacher-centred discipline with a heavy focus on linguistic literacy – reading and writing. But the introduction of multimodal and multimedia texts into the Australian Curriculum: English reshapes our understanding of the English subject. English teachers are now responsible for the teaching of multiliteracies, inviting another challenge for teachers because "literacy must address the impact of new communication technologies, and the texts delivered by them" (Bull and Anstey, 2010, p. 6).

Meeting the demands of changing literacy needs, curriculum changes and the federal 1-1 initiative forces secondary English teachers in Australia to reconsider their pedagogy. Project Based Learning (PBL) is a methodology that will provide teachers with a scaffold to integrate digital technologies and multiliteracies into the English classroom. This humble book hopes to support English teachers as they take steps towards modifying their practice to meet the exciting, yet challenging changes with which they are confronted.

REFERENCES:

Barron, B. & Darling-Hammond, L. (2008). Teaching for meaningful learning: A review of research on inquiry-based and cooperative learning. In L. Darling-Hammond, Barron, B., Pearson, D., Schoenfeld, A., Stage, E., Zimmerman, T., Cervetti, G. & Tison, J. (Ed.), *Powerful Learning: What We Know About Teaching for Understanding* (pp. 11–70). San Francisco: Jossey-Bass.

Black, P. & Wiliam, D. (1998). Inside the black box: Raising standards through classroom assessment. *Phi Delta Kappan*, 80(2), 139–148.

Bull, G. & Anstey, M. (2010). *Redefining Literacy and Text. Evolving pedagogies: reading and writing in a multi-modal world.* Carlton South, Vic: Education Services Australia.

Cazden, C., Cope, B., Fairclough, N., Gee, J. P., Kress, M., Luke, A., Luke, C., Michaels, S. & Nakata, M. (1996). 'A pedagogy of multiliteracies: designing social futures'. *Harvard Educational Review*, 66(1), 60–92.

Mizuko, I., Horst, H. A., Bittanti, M., Boyd, D., Herr-Stephenson, B., Lange, P. G., Pascoe, C. J. & Robinson, L. (2008). *Living and Learning with New Media: Summary of Findings from the Digital Youth Project. The John D. and Catherine T. MacArthur Foundation Reports on Digital Media and Learning*, November 2008.

HOW DOES PBL RUN IN THE ENGLISH CLASSROOM?

There are five key components that we include in every project to ensure successful student engagement and deep learning. These are *a driving question, a project outline, an expert, a hook lesson* and *a project wall*. These elements will help you to structure each project and to keep students focused on their learning goals. The following pages provide further detail about each of these core elements.

DRIVING QUESTION

This term was developed by the Buck Institute for Education (BIE, 2014) and is fundamental to every project. A driving question (sometimes referred to as an essential question) is an open-ended question which forms the basis for the inquiry which takes place throughout the project.

As PBL is fundamentally an inquiry-based approach to teaching and learning, the driving question is the motivating force behind every project. It is the basis of all inquiry throughout the project, "driving" what students will need to know and do along the way.

A driving question is like the foundations of a building or the launchpad for a space mission. Everything starts from there. Driving questions also provide focus for learners: What are we trying to learn? How do we go about answering the question? What do we need to know, make and do? How do we demonstrate our learning?

Driving questions should be open-ended and not something that can be answered simply by picking up an encyclopaedia, textbook or by an internet search. This ensures that students will need to engage in extended inquiry to complete the project. It is often helpful to embed the content focus and final product within the driving question in order to help students understand what they are heading towards as they progress through the project. Wherever possible, educators should consider how to leave the product open to student choice and personal preference, and therefore ownership over the product that eventually comes to light. It is also a good idea to include the audience for whom your learners will be creating within the driving question. Here are some driving questions from our book *Are Humans Wild at Heart? And Other Epic English Projects for Years 9–10* (Hawker Brownlow Education, 2016):

How can one voice change the world?
How can we support teenagers who are finding life hard?
Why do emos write poetry?
How can we design a winning advertising campaign for a production of Macbeth?
What makes a story worth stealing?

PROJECT OUTLINE

A project outline is a document explaining the rationale and aims, audience, products and learning intentions of each project. These can be handed out to students to be put into their project packets (explained later), laminated and posted on to the classroom project wall (explained later), or both. If you have access to laptops, PCs or tablets, you might like to create a digital project outline using Google Docs, Weebly or Canvas.

Project outlines provide students with an idea of what they will be learning, the products they will be making and for what audience, and the steps they need to be taking along the way in order to successfully complete the project. Project outlines serve a dual purpose – they help students with project management and understand learning expectations, and they are also great for the teacher as a formative assessment tool. The Discover, Create, Share structure enables the process of the project to be broken down into manageable steps so each student or team of students' progress can be tracked at each stage.

An effective project outline should do the following things.

- *Be visually appealing.* No-one wants to be given a boring document that basically explains what will be happening in class along with the work that needs to be done in order to pass the required assessments. Visually appealing project outlines are more likely to engage students with what they're doing, plus they look great on your classroom project wall.
- *Clearly display the driving question.* The driving question is one of the main motivators behind any good project. By having it clearly displayed on the project outline, the class can constantly refer back to it and assess how they are progressing along the way to answering it. There are usually a number of related questions, guided by the Need to Knows of the project, and it is quite useful to include these on the outline to help guide students along the way.
- *Clearly outline the process, products and audience of the project.* Projects can usually be broken down into three distinct phases: an initial inquiry or Discover phase in which students engage in extensive research around a particular topic; an additional production stage in which students Create some sort of product for their intended audience; and a final stage in which they prepare to present or Share their product with the audience.

NEED TO KNOW

This is an essential stage of the project where students are given an opportunity to identify their prior knowledge and to begin their inquiry process. The goal of this stage is to have students who can confidently articulate what they already *know* that will help them succeed and to thoughtfully identify what they still *need to know* to be successful. The Know and Need to Know can be categorised in this way: skills (e.g. how to write a short story, how to edit a film or how to deliver an effective speech), content knowledge (e.g. the five elements of narrative, William Shakespeare's biography, the plot of *The Catcher in the Rye* by J.D. Salinger [1951]) and basic information about the project (e.g. how many students in a team, what the driving question is, who the public audience will be). As you can tell, this process is grounded in the much-loved KW(H)L table (see an example on page 149). It helps to have students understand that what they *know* should be phrased as statements, and what they *need to know* should be phrased as questions. This process is required for all projects, as it forces students to think critically about their prior knowledge and skills, as well as generating a whole range of questions to help them launch their inquiry. You can use a KW(H)L table for this or have students sit in teams and generate a list of five things they definitely need to know in order to be successful with the project. This is a sneaky activity because often you, as the teacher, know what kinds of things they will identify – but that's what differentiates the typical classroom experience from the PBL experience. It's about students actively identifying what they need to know and how they will discover that. We love putting these questions up on the project wall and returning to them each week to monitor learning – students like being able to cross questions off the list and it helps them see that they are learning. Below is a list of different strategies that you can use to support students' generation of questions they need to answer during the project.

- After you have given students the project outline, have them turn it over and rule up a KW(H)L table on the back. As them to write at least five "what I know" statements in the K column, and at least five "what I need to know" questions in the W column. If they feel confident, they can identify "How I will discover the answers" in the H column for each of the questions in their W column. Then, have students take turns reading out their K and W columns, one statement or question at a time. If students have the same Know or Need to Know as others, they put an asterisk beside it. As students share, allocate a student to be the note-taker (or you can do this yourself) and have all of the ideas added to a class KW(H)L table. This sharing continues around the class until all possible statements and questions have been added. Sometimes we vary this by having all students standing up, and then once their ideas are all added they sit down – the last student standing is the one with the most inquiring mind.

- Speed KWLing: This is a variation on speed dating that we have used successfully many times whereby the aim is for students to share the ideas they have added to the K and W columns of their KWL table. The students sit in two circles; the circle in the middle moves, and the one on outside stays put. Students have to select TWO questions from their "Wonder/Want to Know" column and share these with the person sitting in front of them until the teacher says stop. If the Need to Know is new, they add it to their own KWL chart. If not, they just discuss how they will find the answer to their question through sources and/or experts. Once all students have paired up, the teacher leads a whole-class discussion about the students' list of Need to Know questions, and how they might work in teams to answer their questions. The list is typed up and put on the project wall – this is the basis of their project "investigation" phase.

- Students are given different coloured Post-Its and are asked on one colour to identify everything they *know* that will help them with the project (skills, content knowledge, project elements) On the other colour, they record all the questions to which they *need* answers in order to be successful with the project (skills, content knowledge, project stuff). When they have filled at least five Post-Its for each, have students stick them to a big KW(H)L table on the wall. Ask two students to read through the Know statements and Need to Know questions while you type them up in a program like Google Docs. With the Knows, if they are very specific skills that can benefit the others in the group, you can add the student's name beside the skill, e.g. *Duncan is proficient in four coding languages*. With the Need to Know questions, give students 10 minutes to identify HOW they might find the answer to the question. At this stage, you might like to speak briefly about the need for students to triangulate their information, and to use a range of unusual and unique sources on top of the typical ones (this comes from the BIE creative thinking rubric). By the end of this session, students should have some great inquiry questions, and also have identified some good potential sources.

- Midway through the project (perhaps at the beginning of the Create stage and again at the beginning of the Share stage), have each team decide on five things they still need to know, and also any new things they've discovered they need to know as they move to this next phase of the project. For example, when the project was first introduced, a team might have had this as their Need to Know question: *What type of product will we create to advocate for equality within our school?* But by the time they move into the Create stage, they have decided to create a flash mob; so now they have a lot of questions about flash mobs to which they need to find answers.

- As you can see, Need to Know questions are an excellent formative assessment strategy. But they can also be used as a summative assessment strategy. At the end of a project, give students a quiz where they must write answers to the top 20 Need to Know questions identified at the beginning of the project. This can be done informally, with students calling out when they know the answer, or formally, with students sitting in a large circle and taking turns to answer the questions.

EXPERT/ROCK STAR

This step is probably one of the most daunting of PBL. It requires you to reach out to a complete stranger and ask them to do you a favour – and most often, free of charge. We use the term "rock star" to refer to people who have been invited to participate in a project in the role of "expert" or "audience". This term was coined by the Buck Institute for Education in their fantastic YouTube video, *Project Based Learning: Explained* at **https://www.youtube.com/watch?v=LMCZvGesRz8**. It is always great if someone can fill both roles – coming in early to support the students' initial inquiry, and then returning later to provide students with feedback (and praise) on their final product and/or presentation. Throughout the sample projects you will find suggestions on how to be successful at finding your rock star. Remember that energetic, fun and engaging invitations (from students or from you) are more likely to have a positive response.

HOOK LESSONS

The hook lesson might just be the most fun part of any project. The hook lesson comes at the very beginning of a project. It is sometimes referred to as an entry event or project launch. The idea is to hook your students' interest in an idea, form, problem or text. It also aims to initiate inquiry. A hook might be the length of your regular English lesson, or it might be a whole-day or half-day event or excursion. A hook lesson should be high-energy, fun, challenging and engaging enough to get your students starting to ask questions about the project and interested enough to want to learn more.

When planning your hook lesson, you need to think about what you believe your students will find the most interesting about your project – whether that be modern adaptations of literary classics or how far a grenade could be thrown in the First World War. One easy way of doing this is by making connections between the themes in a text and your students' lives. For example, Shakespeare's Romeo and Juliet can be linked to the students' experiences of falling in love, struggling to choose between friendship groups, the pressures of family expectations or fighting with their parents. Now, think about fun ways of hooking students into thinking about these ideas. Students often enjoy games or competing in teams – how could you make the key content and skills of your project obvious through a fun game of trivia?

Each of the sample projects in this book include examples of hook lessons that you may use or adapt to use with your class.

PROJECT WALLS

A project wall is a wall inside the classroom dedicated to the learning that takes place throughout the course of the project. It is a good idea to place the project outline on the project wall, along with the Need to Knows, any rubrics that are being used and of course plenty of examples of student work to display and celebrate their learning. Project walls typically start out quite bare and become increasingly vibrant, bright and colourful throughout the course of the project. By the end of the project, it's quite common to run out of space on your wall. As with project outlines, if you're in a school that has easy access to a lot of technology, you might want to create a digital project wall. We've found that tools like Weebly and Glogster are great for this, but there are many other options as well. This will also be a great option for teachers who don't have access to the same classroom every day. We have also had success with making project walls in common spaces, such as in the corridors outside or near the classroom.

Project walls are a terrific, engaging way for both teachers and students to track their learning throughout the course of the project. Having the driving question and Need to Knows posted on the classroom wall ensures that they are constantly referred back to in order to formatively assess which aspects of the inquiry process have been completed and what else still needs to be learnt. Student work can be showcased on the project wall along with any language features learnt throughout the course of the project. This is useful not only for the project which is currently being undertaken, but also for any future projects and classroom activities in which these language features might be revised or of use.

Project walls are also a great way to celebrate success. As they typically grow throughout the project, it's a great way to look back on how far the class has come and to reflect on the learning. Remember, project walls are about tracking learning, so don't feel the need to only put perfect, completed work on there. Celebrate learning by posting up peer feedback and student drafts. An additional advantage of the project wall is that it brightens up the classroom. We love it when visitors come to our classrooms and see our project walls. It's quite common for them to take pictures of the learning being celebrated on our classroom walls.

There's no exact method for making a project wall. All you need is a blank wall in your classroom. From here you put up your project outline with the driving question and Need to Knows. You then begin to add student work as the class progresses through the project. This would include any language features that the class has been learning, aspects of creative writing or narrative components such as setting, plot and character development, as well as things such as storyboards, artworks and photos of classroom activities. If you use things like Know-Want-Learn (KWL) tables or teamwork rubrics, these can also be placed on the project wall for reference. Project walls are fantastic for revision and reflection.

EXAMPLE PROJECT WALLS

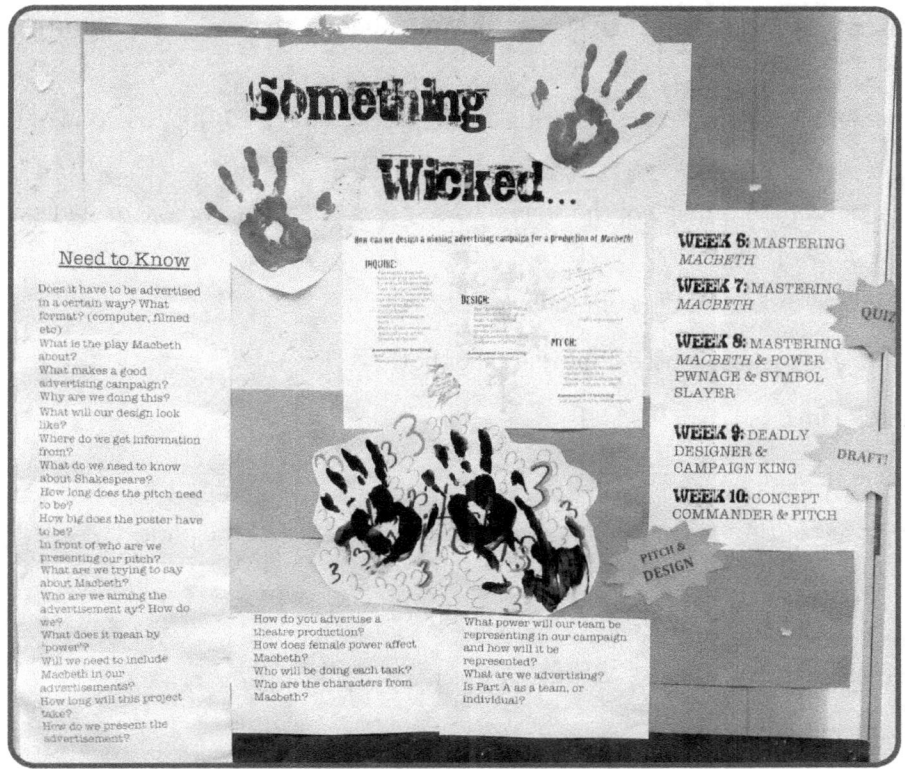

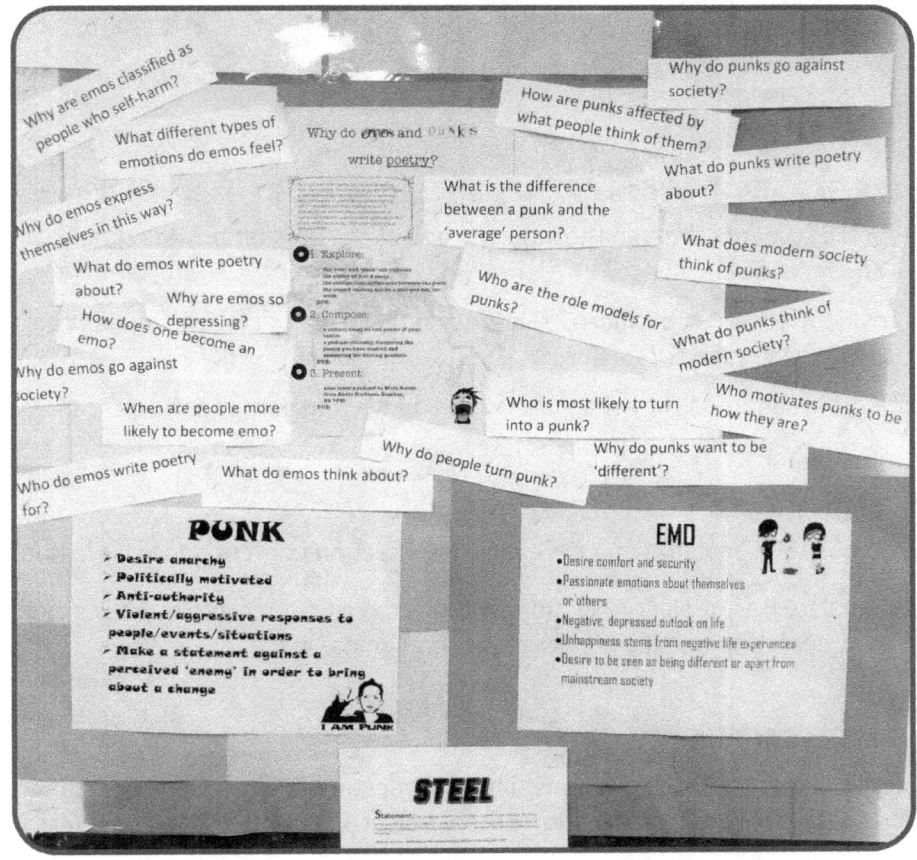

PBL AT A GLANCE

BEFORE THE PROJECT
1. Identify an authentic problem or challenge for your students that connects to the real world and your syllabus content.
2. Design a project using the Project Essentials Checklist (on page 154), or use one of our model projects.
3. Organise experts from outside of the school to be guest speakers, and/or the audience for student work.
4. Create your own project outline or modify one of ours.
5. Organise project packets – hard copy, digital or both.
6. Plan project teams.
7. Create space for a project wall.
8. Gather together quality resources to support the three stages of the project.

LAUNCH THE PROJECT
1. Lead a hook lesson.
2. Hand out the project outline.
3. Establish Need to Know by completing the K and W columns of a KWL table.
4. Set up teams.
5. Create a project calendar.

MANAGE THE PROJECT (SEE THE MORE DETAILED ANATOMY OF A PROJECT ON PAGE 11)
- Discover – guide students through the inquiry stage of the project; providing timely and specific instruction and feedback.
- Create – provide timely and specific instruction and feedback as students create their products or design solutions to identified problems.
- Share – support students as they share their learning with an authentic audience.

REFLECT ON THE PROJECT
1. Students complete "L" column of a KWL table to reflect on content and skills learnt.
2. Students complete post-project reflection – it could be a Socratic circle, focus group, class discussion or blog post, completing specific project reflection questions.

REVISE THE PROJECT
1. Teacher uses student feedback from post-project reflection and their own project evaluation to revise the project's design for the next iteration of the project.

ANATOMY OF A PROJECT

HOOK → NEED TO KNOW → TEAM BUILDING & GOAL-SETTING →

DISCOVER

Problem/Challenge
- What?
- Why?
- Who?
- How?

Teaching and learning may include:
- guided and independent research
- explicit instruction from the teacher
- expert/guest talks
- hands-on experiments/workshops
- student-centred, teacher-designed activities
- analysis and deconstruction of model texts, existing products or solutions
- fieldwork or immersive excursions.

ASSESS

Content: quiz, essay, report, presentation

Skills: collaboration and critical thinking via rubrics and exit slips; time-management and organisation via journal

CREATE

Solution
- Product
- Prototype
- Performance
- Pitch

Teaching and learning may include:
- identifying wants and needs of audience/users
- generating and selecting ideas
- co-construction of product criteria/rubric
- planning, drafting and creating product(s)
- giving, receiving and applying feedback
- seeking support from experts/mentors.

ASSESS

Content: ideation, drafts/prototype, plans, teacher feedback to refine product

Skills: collaboration and creative thinking via rubrics and exit slips; time-management and organisation via journal

SHARE

Audience
- Panel of experts
- Community
- Online
- Family and friends

Teaching and learning may include:
- deconstruction of model presentations
- co-construction of presentation criteria/rubric
- planning and drafting speeches
- creating presentation materials such as slideshows
- practise presentations with peer-feedback
- preparing venue for presentations
- creating invitations and inviting guests
- preparing exhibition materials.

ASSESS

Content: final product, practice and final presentation

Skills: creative thinking and presentation via rubric; time-management and organisation via journal

→ REFLECT

DRIVING QUESTION — SKILLS AND CONTENT

PRACTICE PROJECTS

A great way to develop students' familiarity with the processes inherent to quality PBL is to run one or two microprojects. A microproject is a small problem students must solve, or a product that they must produce. They have only one hour to complete the task before sharing with the class. This activity can also be an effective pre-testing strategy, as it allows you to identify students' capacities to collaborate, think creatively and critically, solve problems, manage their time and present their ideas. Identifying students' strengths and weaknesses before a project starts allows you to more meaningfully create project teams, and to plan activities to develop students' areas for development.

With these microprojects you need to ensure you have all necessary equipment prepared before the lesson, and have it laid out in the room ready for a team member to collect. You should also have the classroom furniture set up for students to work in teams. Begin the lesson by asking students to make a team of four (for these practice projects students can make their own teams), and give each team a copy of the project outline. Read through the outline as a class, and tell them they have 30 or 40 minutes to complete the task (depending on the time you have available – remember you need at least 10 minutes at the end for presentations) as a team. Tell them they will be presenting their finished product to the class in a 60-second pitch or presentation. If you are doing the bridge-building project, students' bridges will be tested in front of the class with progressively heavier weights. Students are then set to work on the project. As they work, walk around the room and take notes on students' teamwork, problem-solving techniques, and creative and critical thinking skills. You may like to use formal rubrics for this; we recommend the BIE K–2 rubrics for this task as they are easy to use in one lesson and not too detailed. The rubrics can be found at *bie.org*.

At the end of this book in the "Additional Resources" section you will find two project outlines for practice projects to run with your students. Furthermore, if you are responsible for running PBL professional development in your school, these project outlines can also be fun to run with teachers to help them better understand the PBL process and required skills.

PROJECT BASED LEARNING AND THE GENERAL CAPABILITIES

NOTE: *While the term "General Capabilities" is specific to our context as Australian teachers (it comes from our national curriculum), the capabilities themselves are relevant to every teacher around the world, as they are essential skills that all students must master to be successful in the 21st century.*

The Australian Curriculum clearly articulates an awareness of the need to change our perceptions of our learners and our practice as teachers. This is articulated through the General Capabilities and the Cross-Curriculum Priorities. The image below presents an overview of the General Capabilities. The central text accurately captures our goal as educators for our students, for each to become a "successful learner, confident and creative individual, and active and informed citizen" (ACARA, 2014). It is our intention to show how each of the General Capabilities aligns with the key elements of Project Based Learning that were identified by the Buck Institute for Education. These eight essentials for PBL are Voice and Choice; Significant Content; In-depth Inquiry; Public Audience; Revision & Reflection; Driving Question; Need to Know and 21st-Century Skills. Where possible, we give examples of how each capability can be targeted in the PBL English classroom. It is our belief that PBL is a methodology that provides students with the opportunity to strengthen, develop and demonstrate each of these capabilities.

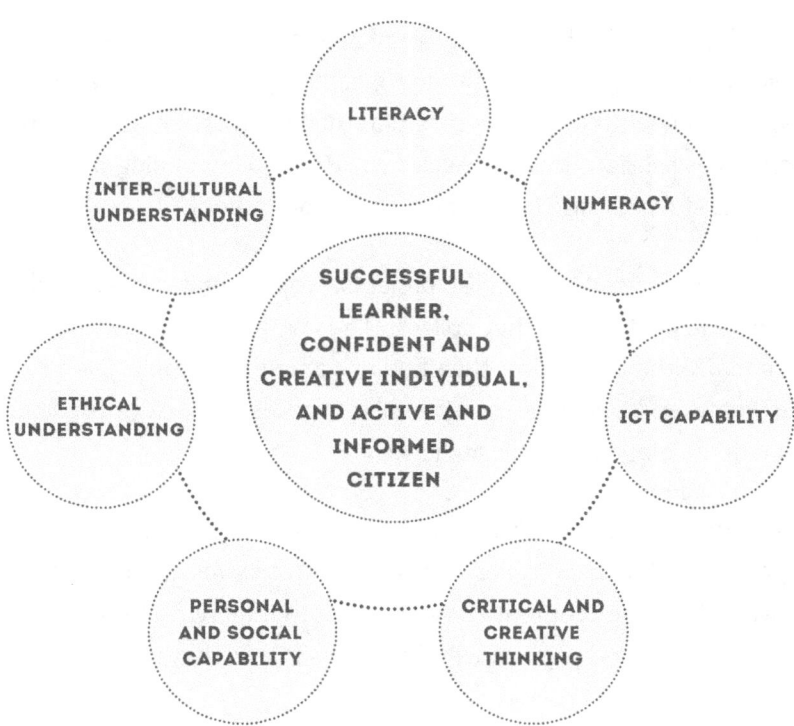

Adapted from: http://australiancurriculum.edu.au/f-10-curriculum/general-capabilities/.

LITERACY

Literacy is the need to know for all young people. Being literate opens the door to the other capabilities. Without literacy, it's very difficult to contribute and participate meaningfully in society. It's not impossible; it's just very difficult. Remember as well that literacy includes visual literacy and critical literacy. During Project Based Learning, literacy is developed through both explicit instruction and through more constructivist, constructionist and collaborative learning strategies.

Furthermore, a key aspect of PBL is the process of planning, drafting, peer/self-assessment and revision. When applied to written or spoken products, this process has a significant impact on students' literacy skills. This process becomes more pertinent for students when they are producing the product for a public audience – online or face to face.

NUMERACY

PBL provides students with the opportunity to think in a more open way about their subjects. The segregating of subjects is an unfortunate consequence of the traditional schooling model. Spend 30 minutes on a bus trip chatting with colleagues from other faculties and you'll discover wonderful connections between your subjects, such as the connections between patterns in English and maths. The moment we stop talking about covering content and we start talking real-world applications of our subjects, we realise the need to see our subjects as interrelated. When we are driven by interest and real-world application, not only does engagement improve, but so too do learning outcomes.

A current global trend is STEM – the integration of the study of Science, Technology, Engineering and Maths. Through multidisciplinary projects, students are mastering STEM skills. Moreover, these projects drive students through a process of in-depth inquiry as they determine what they need to know and how to find out this information or develop these skills. A lot of the skills you develop by running the projects in this book can be used to design and run successful multidisciplinary projects in your school.

Numeracy can also be incorporated into English projects. Projects may require students to conduct in-depth inquiry through surveys and analyse the data they collect. They may also engage with the data collected by others (often accessed online) and use this to support their findings about their topic. Even everyday numeracy comes into play as students estimate and calculate the amount of food and drink needed (and related costs) when planning the presentation of learning to a public audience.

PBL necessitates in-depth inquiry. A significant part of both qualitative and quantitative research is accessing numerical data – be it graphs, statistics or tables. This applies to all subjects. If we don't give our students the opportunity to engage with significant content through in-depth inquiry, we're missing a wonderful chance to allow them to appreciate the power and importance of numbers in everyday life, not just in maths.

INFORMATION AND COMMUNICATION TECHNOLOGY

While PBL isn't about technology (you can easily complete a great project without access to any technology) it certainly is enhanced by access to a range of information and communication technologies (ICTs). During PBL, ICT capability develops naturally as part of the students' learning. But it's not about learning to use a particular online tool or program just for the sake of it, or because it might make boring work a little bit more engaging. The early stage of all projects is in-depth inquiry – this is the stage where students are driven by deep, personally developed questions about the project. Like everyone in the 21st century, students will begin their research on the internet. This phase gives teachers a wonderful opportunity to model effective research skills and the importance of curating information using a variety of online tools (social bookmarking sites and tools like Pinterest and Scoop.it are popular at this stage). Students learn these skills not because the teacher has determined it's good for them, they learn them because they need to know them in order to be successful with their project.

Collaboration and communication are key to PBL because students spend most of their time working in small teams. We're told so often that these are *the* 21st-century skills for young people to master. The workforce is collaborative and globalised; our students need to be able to work in a team and to communicate effectively with anyone, anywhere and at any time. This is where an online classroom is essential – not as a space where resources are accessed, but rather as a space where students can collaborate and communicate whenever they need to. Edmodo is an excellent tool for this purpose. This social network for education allows students to develop their digital citizenship (communicating with courtesy, compassion and clarity) under the eye of their teacher and they can communicate with their teams whenever they need to. Teachers can easily assess the development of these 21st-century skills and quickly give feedback to praise good behaviours and redirect negative behaviours.

ICTs play a big part in the revision and reflection process of PBL. In all projects, students are required to draft and revise their work. This process is enhanced through the use of tools like Google Docs (great for collaborative writing and planning) and more familiar programs like Microsoft Word, where students can use track changes and comments to illustrate their revisions. One of the core routines of PBL is goal-setting and reflecting on learning. This process can be done in a workbook, but it's far more effective when it's done using blogs or a site like Edmodo. Blogging throughout a project allows students to appreciate that learning is a process and that improvement happens over time. Blogging gives students a place to voice their concerns about the project as well as the joy of successfully solving a problem or creating something amazing.

Finally, the most obvious use of ICTs during PBL is for creating the product and accessing a public audience. Allowing students to have a voice and a choice as part of a project is essential to ensure engagement and relevance of learning. This voice and choice typically comes into play around the product that teams will be producing to demonstrate their learning. Your students might choose from a range of forms, some including ICTs, such as videos, websites and online magazines. You might enjoy setting a challenge for your students, so they need to create a type of text they know nothing about, forcing them to develop their ICT capabilities. This can make some students uncomfortable because they're really being pushed, but if you're there to provide support just in time, then this is a great opportunity for mastering responsible risk-taking. Your students will enjoy creating cool products such as websites, podcasts, short films and online fiction – things they might not normally get the opportunity to make in English.

Of course, these products would mean nothing if they didn't have an authentic, public audience. Teachers are time-poor (and our students are too), so having access to an online audience rather than an after-school audience of mums and dads can be really helpful. One great thing to do is to connect with another class from somewhere else in the world – even if it's just the primary school 40 minutes away. Today there is a range of technologies at our disposal that can facilitate this connection – Skype, Edmodo and YouTube are just a few examples. If connecting with another class sounds too risky for you, do a bit of networking and see if you can get a guest expert to Skype in to hear your students' final presentations. Our young people need these experiences – their learning should not be confined to the four walls of the classroom.

CRITICAL AND CREATIVE THINKING

Critical and creative thinking are lifelong skills that all people should master. It's this type of thinking that can lead to a happy and successful life. Of course, teaching critical and creative thinking skills is a conundrum to teachers who feel pressured to cover a lot of content. Luckily for people using PBL as their main teaching method, critical and creative thinking is much easier to develop and refine.

As you will have noticed, the English projects in this book are broken down into three main parts: inquiry/discovery/research, create/compose/produce and present/promote. Of course, the first part of the project doesn't really stop; inquiry is an iterative process and necessary at all stages. It is important to use a lot of visible thinking strategies at all stages of PBL, as these develop and strengthen critical and creative thinking. Making your thinking visible is an important 21st-century skill. This type of thinking is new, but it is extremely important in our world today as our problems become more complex and more immediate. Strong critical and creative thinking is necessary if our young people are to thrive in our ridiculously fast 21st-century world. If we spend time making thinking visible – showcasing to ourselves and our peers what we're thinking, how we're thinking and why we're thinking like that about a topic, product, etc. – then we are valuing critical and creative thinking; we're having conversations about it in class. This is a way of empowering our young people to see that they *can* and *do* think this way.

Through PBL in the English classroom, your students will develop their creative thinking through composing and designing products like podcasts, websites, rap battles, narrative poetry, collaborative novellas, machinima, short films and anthologies of personal essays. This process is predicated on revision and reflection. There are many visible thinking strategies for brainstorming and planning of which your students can take advantage. These include star-bursting, KWL tables, think/pair/share, think/puzzle/explore and mind-mapping on portable whiteboards. Another excellent creative thinking activity is whole-group "what if" question-asking when students present plans or drafts of their work to their peers.

As previously mentioned, projects necessitate in-depth inquiry. Students are developing their critical thinking as they learn to curate information found on the internet (and sometimes even in books). There are lots of protocols available to support students in their ability to judge the quality, credibility and relevance of information that they find on the web. PBL means that students aren't being taught these skills in a "one-off" lesson, rather they are using these methods time and time again at the beginning stages of their projects. We need to have young people who are critical of the content that is delivered to them via the media. This is essential in a media-rich age where consumerism has become the natural state for our young people. A great activity is to actually teach students how to use Google effectively – people expect that this knowledge and skill is a given among young people. Another strategy that encourages critical thinking is the question-formulating technique (QFT). This is a strategy that supports students in their question-asking as they learn to identify open and closed questions and how to develop the best questions to ask. The QFT has resulted in some great questions which students have made visible to their peers through writing with whiteboard markers on windows and displaying questions on the walls of the classroom.

Finally, giving students the freedom to pursue their interests in projects (even if all you feel you can allow is choice in product or audience) allows them to think more deeply about their own passions. Passions are *the* drivers of creative and critical thinking. There are a number of stages within PBL where students can be given a voice and ask: What is the significance of the topic to their lives? What are their concerns about the topic? Are teachers missing something pertinent to them as human beings?. Two of these stages are the crafting of the driving question and their daily reflections on their feelings about the project and their learning. To discover students' interests you could do one of these activities:

- Ask students to write you a letter introducing themselves.
- Ask students to list the five things most important to them in their lives.
- Sit students in a circle and have them take turns to share ideas based on their favourite ways to learn, favourite activities or what they want to do when they leave school.
- Get your students passion-blogging once a week about what they value the most right now.

PERSONAL AND SOCIAL CAPABILITY

All teachers want their students to go off and live happy and successful lives. But just what successful means and looks like varies significantly between our young people. This is something that we, as teachers, need to accept. Success for many of our students is simply to be happy and healthy, to feel safe and to feel valued. This capability is great because it requires teachers to see the human being behind the student.

This capability is about considering how our young people are developing emotionally and socially. It's about being great role models and facilitating learning experiences that ensure these young people are being given the opportunity to develop their *self-awareness, self-management, social awareness* and *social management* (these are the four elements of Personal and Social Capability as outlined in the Australian Curriculum document). According to the Australian Curriculum: General Capabilities, if you just teach the document, students will develop all of these aspects of personal and social capability. We firmly believe that through PBL, students can most effectively develop these capabilities.

The best type of PBL is real-world and authentic. As renowned PBL author Suzie Boss says, PBL gives students the opportunity to contribute to and change (even slightly) their world. Boss says all projects should target one of the three As: action, awareness and advocacy. Essentially, if a project is going to be significant, engaging and valuable, it will allow students to develop a sense of themselves and their role within their local and wider community. Students will work on real-world problems in their community or wider society (such as transport issues, employment, youth homelessness, environment issues, bullying, depression, etc.) and contribute to solving these problems in some way. By giving our young people a voice through seeking a public audience for their learning, their compositions and their concerns, we are helping them to develop a better sense of themselves as active and effective contributors to their local and global communities.

ETHICAL UNDERSTANDING

According to the Australian Curriculum, "Ethical understanding involves students in building a strong personal and socially oriented ethical outlook that helps them to manage context, conflict and uncertainty, and to develop an awareness of the influence that their values and behaviour have on others" (ACARA, 2014a). In secondary school we are often working with young people who simply lack resilience or a deep appreciation for their own values and how these can impact those around them. Why? Because they are young people finding their place within the world. But maybe it's also because they don't understand or can't appreciate the relevance of what they are doing RIGHT NOW in their school lives. To teenagers, school can often seem like they're in a holding pen waiting until they're given the chance to be morally responsible. In order to support our students to develop "personal values and attributes such as honesty, resilience, empathy and respect for others" (*Melbourne Declaration on Education Goals for Young Australians*, 2008), we need to create learning experiences that foster and nurture these values and attributes.

PBL is about problem-finding and problem-solving. Not the problems in the back of the book, or the imaginary problems identified in a novel, but the REAL problems of our world that need addressing. It is in the driving question of a project that we see the centrality of problems. These problems might be based in the class (*How can we design a learning space that supports the needs of all learners?*), school (*Can we, as students, prevent bullying in our school?*), local community (*How can we educate our community about the impact that individuals' decisions have on others?*), national (*Can we create a short film that will change politician's attitudes towards climate change?*) or global (*How can poetry be used to inspire people to donate money to combat the global food crisis?*). The best problems, of course, are those identified by students through their own personal experience or through their own in-depth inquiry. To help students with their problem-finding, you could use this sentence from the Australian Curriculum as stimulus for discussion and brainstorming: "Complex issues require responses that take account of ethical considerations such as human rights and responsibilities, animal rights, environmental issues and global justice."

(ACARA, 2014a.) It simply is NOT enough to just have our students writing persuasive speeches, research articles or poems about these issues, handing them in to their teacher for a mark and ticking a box. We MUST empower our young people to actively take part in making a contribution to their world – to contribute their ideas to solving complex problems. This means ensuring that their learning has a public audience.

Of course, we can't expect one class doing PBL to solve the world's problems – but many hands make light work. According to the Australian Curriculum, "Technologies bring local and distant communities into classrooms, exposing students to knowledge and global concerns as never before." (ACARA, 2014a.) With the capacity to bring others into our classroom via Skype, Edmodo, social media, etc., we have the capacity to work together towards incremental changes to our problematic world. Giving students a taste of their own personal agency and allowing them to develop their understanding of themselves as ethical human beings is central to our jobs as teachers.

INTERCULTURAL UNDERSTANDING

For the Australian Curriculum, intercultural understanding "assists young people to become responsible local and global citizens, equipped through their education for living and working together in an interconnected world." (ACARA, 2014b.)

Creating learning experiences that provide students with the opportunity to connect and collaborate with students from backgrounds different from their own truly does nurture intercultural understanding. During PBL, students develop essential 21st-century skills as they establish connections with other schools or with experts from outside of school. PBL provides the students with "the ability to relate to and communicate across cultures at local, regional and global levels" (ACARA, 2014c).

Using this approach to learning truly opens our eyes, as teachers, to the potential connections our young people can make with others. It doesn't have to be connections from outside of the school; intercultural connections within schools are just as worthwhile.

It is essential that we continue to value our young people as the future of our world and support them as best we can to develop or strengthen these important attributes of good humans. We truly do feel that an approach to learning such as PBL that is experiential, authentic and engaging provides our learners with the BEST opportunity to hone these very important values and attributes.

RESOURCES

Australian Curriculum, Assessment and Reporting Authority (ACARA), 2014. *General Capabilities* [online]. Available at: http://australiancurriculum.edu.au/f-10-curriculum/general-capabilities/. Accessed 07/12/2017.

Australian Curriculum, Assessment and Reporting Authority (ACARA), 2014a. *Ethical Understanding* [online]. Available at: http://australiancurriculum.edu.au/f-10-curriculum/general-capabilities/ethical-understanding/. Accessed 13/11/2017.

Australian Curriculum, Assessment and Reporting Authority (ACARA), 2014b. *Intercultural Understanding* [online]. Available at: http://australiancurriculum.edu.au/f-10-curriculum/general-capabilities/intercultural-understanding/. Accessed 13/11/2017.

Australian Curriculum, Assessment and Reporting Authority (ACARA), 2014c. *Version 7.5: Intercultural Understanding: Introduction* [online]. Available at: http://v7-5.australiancurriculum.edu.au/generalcapabilities/intercultural-understanding/introduction/introduction. Accessed 13/11/2017. Please note that this link was active at the time of publication.

Ministerial Council on Education, Employment, Training and Youth Affairs (2008). First Edition. [PDF] Melbourne. *Melbourne Declaration on Education Goals for Young Australians.* Page 9. Available at: http://www.curriculum.edu.au/verve/_resources/National_Declaration_on_the_Educational_Goals_for_Young_Australians.pdf. Accessed 13/11/2017.

A WORD ABOUT PBL AND ASSESSMENT

Assessment is an integral part of Project Based Learning. It sees learning as an ongoing process and, as a result, champions the use of formative assessment strategies that help students identify learning goals and the strategies to achieve them. Our three-stage approach to PBL has been designed with assessment in mind. Student learning is assessed at each of the stages using a range of strategies. For each sample project, we have included suggested strategies for assessment at each of these three stages of learning. Our preference is that marks are not given for project work (see explanation below), however, how you choose to formally assess your students will be dependent on your school's assessment policy and your own personal beliefs.

Our approach to PBL is all about the process. It makes PBL slower and messier and may sometimes "look" less successful than those cool videos you see of successful PBL projects on YouTube. But this is okay with us because our focus is learning and the process *is* the learning. One of the most effective types of assessment is peer assessment. The scariest thing for teachers when implementing peer assessment is the time that it takes to "perfect". Students simply don't have the skill set to effectively assess the work of themselves or their peers. They need to be taught how to do this – they need support and modelling. They need to be fully involved in the process, but most of all they need to be given time. Time? It's the one thing most teachers feel they don't have enough of, but we have to let go of our focus on content and reclaim the higher ground and TEACH SKILLS. Luckily for us English teachers we have this built directly into the Australian Curriculum: English (2014).

We were influenced in the design of our scaffolds for peer and self-assessment by the work of Geoff Petty, a leading expert on teaching methods. We think he's great because he has so many wonderful resources for free online. Type his name into Google and you will find them. Petty argues that too much of the feedback we give students is BACKWARD looking and often this feedback is quantitative (numerical, e.g. 7/10; 70%). But even qualitative feedback (words: e.g. "You didn't begin your sentences with a capital letter.") more often than not looks backwards at what WAS or WASN'T done. Petty advocates for a method of feedback that is both backwards and forwards looking. To do that he uses the "goals, medals and missions" protocol, which you will notice on the checklists we've included in each project. It's great because the language is accessible to all age groups and it is non-threatening. Essentially the "goals" are the criteria for the product (be it a short film, an essay or a presentation) and the "medals" are what has been achieved (this is the backward-looking stuff) and always takes the form of positive statements, e.g. "Your introduction is strong". The "missions" are the important part of the protocol – this is "feed-forward" as it is looking at what the student needs to work on to improve the product or the next product.

When introducing the idea of "feedback" and "feed-forward" to students, it will probably take a little while for them to understand it. Try using a real-world example. Say you're five years old and your dad and teenage brother take you to the park to teach you how to ride your bike without training wheels. Your dad gives you a push, you pedal for a bit and then fall into a bush. Your brother calls out, "Er, you loser! You fell into the bush!" and your dad stands there holding up a sign with the number three on it. That is all the feedback you receive – one is qualitative and one is quantitative. What is your response? You kick your bike and you storm off. No more bike-riding for you, it's too hard and you're terrible at it – the feedback of your loved ones told you so. But what if the imaginary dad did something different? What if he gave a medal for what the child did (the feedback), saying something like, "You managed to stay upright for two metres"? What if he then gave his child a mission (feed-forward), saying something like, "Next time I want you to pedal a bit faster, keep your weight in the middle and avoid leaning to the right"? Sounds like what every dad would do, right? This is "real-world" feedback, but it's not always classroom-world feedback. I'm sure your students will understand that analogy.

To our students, we try to avoid the term "peer assessment". We prefer "peer feedback". The word *assessment* is scary and doesn't reflect the learning that is inherent in this process, rather it focuses more on judgement. A good tip is to get your students to develop the criteria for a product or presentation with you. Write learning goals up on the board, negotiate how to express them and then add them to the checklist template given at the end of this book. We suggest that you phrase the criteria as questions and avoid using the word "student" if possible, as it's preferable to refer to students as writers, essayists, reviewers, filmmakers, etc. This distances the students from feeling like it is a personal criticism being given. What we've discovered is that students need to provide evidence for their feedback – if they only have to tick boxes, they can easily do this randomly and without thought. If you look at the checklist on page 32, you'll see that beside each point in the criteria (the "goals") has a number beside it. This number is a kind of "code" that students use to annotate the work being "assessed". We encourage students to add a cross or tick beside the number so the writer can identify if they have or haven't met that criteria in a specific place. We tell students that they must resist writing corrections on the work (such as spelling and punctuation), as we want to encourage thoughtful revision and independence. We don't want students that need teachers to rewrite their work for them. Students are also required to give written feedback in the form of medals and missions – these must be written in sentences and use the language of the criteria. We have had a lot of success with this approach to assessment, and we hope you will too.

Often the assessment we have in our schools doesn't actually assess the real learning gains students make. Too often assessment is summative, assessing the end product of learning and not the process. We believe this is problematic. The biggest problem with summative assessment is that it does not give students the feedback they need to improve. If students fail to be provided with opportunities for teacher, peer and self-feedback throughout the learning cycle, students easily become disengaged, demotivated and continue to make the same errors unchecked. Of course, another problem of summative assessment is the failure to assess those skills that have been dubbed "21st-century skills". These skills include cooperation, critical and creative thinking, and the ability to use digital technologies to enhance learning, collaboration, presentation skills, problem-solving, curiosity, ethical thinking and persistence. All of these things are essential to being a thriving, successful individual today. These things have not been formally assessed as long as we have been teaching but this, thankfully, is changing in many schools. We believe assessing these skills is important to support student learning.

Built in to quality PBL is a series of investigations, products and a final presentation of learning. Each task involves teacher, peer and self-feedback. Students actively engage in goal-setting and reflection tasks. This is authentic learning. Assessment is a massive driver of teaching and learning – we can't ignore it.

PART TWO
SAMPLE PROJECTS

YEAR 7:

1. GAME 2 LEARN
2. #LOVEOZYA
3. SUSTAINABLE NEWS
4. READING REIMAGINED
5. ACTING UP!

YEAR 8:

1. BODACIOUS BALLADEERS
2. AWESOME AUTEURS
3. LIFE STORIES
4. SOULE OF THE AGE
5. STEAMPUNK STORIES

YEAR 7

1. GAME 2 LEARN

PROJECT AT A GLANCE:

 **DRIVING QUESTION:** Should video games be used to help us learn in secondary school?

 DISCOVER: Students will research the positive uses of video games in the classroom as well as the negative consequences of video games in the classroom. They will discover the language features and structure of persuasive texts.

 CREATE: Students will write and film a review of a video game. They will also write a speech that argues for or against the use of video games for learning in secondary school.

 SHARE: Students will publish their video game review to YouTube and present their speeches before the school principal. Take it further: Consider making this a cross-curricular project by connecting with a media or multimedia class and have students design and create educational video games. Students might want to design a unit of work that centres on a video game as a model for teachers.

 ASSESSMENT: There are two main assessments for this project: the review of a video game and a speech. Students should be assessed formatively on the plan and draft of each. Undertake summative assessment on the final version of both.

 21ST-CENTURY SKILLS: creative and critical thinking, presentation skills, ICT, collaboration

LITERACY: grammar – sentence types, clauses; punctuation – semicolons, commas, ellipses, dashes and brackets; and reading – summarising and visualising

TYPE OF TEXT: persuasive

LANGUAGE FEATURES OF TEXTS: written: modality, connectives, emotive and figurative language, construction of an argument; visual: shots, angles, editing, lighting, camera movement, sound effects

POSSIBLE TEXTS: There is a wide range of TED and TEDx talks available via YouTube that will provide students with a good model for their speech. ABC television shows such as *Good Game: Spawn Point*, *At the Movies* and *The Book Club*, which can be found on YouTube, are great examples of live reviews.

SHOULD VIDEO GAMES BE USED TO HELP US LEARN IN SECONDARY SCHOOL?

RESEARCH:
- the positive uses of video games in the classroom
- the negative consequences of video games in the classroom
- the design elements of video games
- the language features and structure of persuasive writing.

ASSESSMENT: critical thinking

COMPOSE:
- a video game review
- a piece of writing that argues for or against the use of video games for learning in secondary school.

ASSESSMENT: creative thinking

SHARE:
- your video game review on YouTube
- your answer to the driving question with your principal.

ASSESSMENT: presentation skills

REPRODUCIBLE – PART TWO: SAMPLE PROJECTS YEAR 7 – 1. GAME 2 LEARN

BEFORE YOU BEGIN

CONTACT EXPERTS/ROCK STARS

This project requires your students to present their arguments about video games in front of the school principal, but this could also include gaming or education experts. You may choose to give your students a choice about who they would also like to be in the audience, or you might find it more effective to specify the audience for them. If you choose to specify the audience and include guests from outside of the school, you will likely need to organise invitations to go out quite early in the project, if not before the project begins.

This project also requires students to write and film a review of a video game of their choice. In order to make this part of the project engaging, you might wish to invite in an expert to speak about persuasive writing, developing an argument or contemporary responses to video games. Academics, bloggers or game designers would be an excellent choice for this role.

MODIFY PROJECT OUTLINE

Look at the sample project outline given. Remember that PBL is all about engaging students through making content significant for their needs and interests, so you may wish to make your own project outline or modify ours. You will also need to modify the project outline to indicate due dates for formative and summative assessment.

ORGANISE PROJECT PACKETS

This is an important organisation strategy that we use a lot in PBL. For this project, students will be working in small teams. A project packet is essentially a small folder or document wallet given to each team that contains all of the essential materials for students to be successful with the project. These remain in the classroom and are accessed by students each lesson. Of course, there are so many technology options available that mean that your project packets do not need to be paper-based. The benefits of having digital project packets and ePortfolios means that students can add to and access them when they're at home, and so can you. Some of the online tools that would be great for this application include: Google Drive, Blackboard, Edmodo, Glogster, Weebly, Evernote and Canvas.

PLAN PROJECT TEAMS

Planning teams is inherently difficult, as you must consider the personality as well as the skill level of each student in your class. For this project, it is best to select a mixed team, taking into consideration the following skills: knowledge of video games, public speaking, video-editing skills, communication and creativity. Try to balance the teams to ensure that you have even numbers of outgoing and reserved students. Speaking in front of an audience is daunting for many students. Add to that having the principal in the audience, and students are going to need to feel very supported and comfortable. As such, try to ensure each student has at least one person they trust and are on friendly terms with in their team.

CREATE SPACE FOR A PROJECT WALL

This project wall will need to be updated regularly so students can see their understanding of persuasive texts grow. Start your project wall with the title of the project, "Game 2 Learn". Let your students know this is a pun! In equally large writing, put up your project's driving question – students need to see this as it will drive them through the project and inspire them to think critically. You will also need an A3 colour printout of the project outline. Leave space for a project calendar (or put up a blank one and have a student fill it in as you negotiate due dates etc.), the Need to Know list of questions and a good amount of space for "key terms". Since this is a project that deconstructs video games as texts, it won't take long to identify new words and terms that students previously did not know. Remember that these spaces need to be blank at the beginning of the project, as this information will be added by students during the Discover stage of learning. Use as much colour as you can, because it is important that students are attracted to it, as it is a visible record of their learning. You might even like to nominate a student to be responsible for adding new information to the "key terms" or Need to Know spaces. If you don't happen to have your own classroom, and therefore you can't add information to a wall, how about creating a digital project wall? Online tools like Glogster, Weebly and Canvas are great for this purpose.

LAUNCH YOUR PROJECT

HOOK LESSON

There are so many possibilities for how to hook your students' interest in this project. The first thing to consider is what the main conceptual focus of the project is; in this instance, it could be persuasion or learning. Another approach may focus on video games as texts. Finally, you might decide to focus on the type of product to be created; for this project, it's a speech and a video game review. Some hook lessons based on these approaches might be:

- thirty-second speeches on silly topics like "Vegemite is the best toothpaste", "Sharks make the best pets" or "Crawling is better than walking"
- mini debates on topics such as "Video games teach us nothing" and "Reality television kills your brain"
- playing a range of board games for young children and giving improvised reviews
- a game of trivia where students answer questions about video games.

POSE DRIVING QUESTION

The lesson after the "hook lesson" is very, very important. This is the lesson where students are given access to the project's driving question for the first time. This project's driving question is: *Should video games be used to help us learn in secondary school?*

Of course, it's also a great activity to get students to design the project's driving question with you. This can be done through a class discussion. We have done this a number of times with our classes and it is always surprising what students come up with. When they have ownership over part of the project design, they feel ownership of their learning.

Once you pose this question to the students (we often put it up on the whiteboard or the interactive whiteboard), get each individual to immediately write down their own unmediated personal response to it. This will become their "hypothesis", which will be tested and reshaped as they work through the Discover learning stage.

HAND OUT PROJECT OUTLINE

We recommend that the project outline is printed off in colour or printed onto coloured paper. This sets it apart from other pieces of paper that students will receive or use during the project. The project outline is a very important document as it acts as a flyer for learning. As soon as you hand the project outline out, have students sit quietly and read through it, using a pen or highlighter to identify any information that they feel they do not understand or that they have questions about. This is an essential step, as this information becomes part of what the class has identified as what they need to know. It is a good idea to encourage students to keep this project outline in their team's project packet or their own personal portfolio. We have had great success with students keeping a personal plastic sleeve folder as their "learning portfolio". If you have access to devices like PCs, tablets or laptops you might consider having students create digital portfolios using programs like Google Drive. They will use this for the entire year of projects.

ESTABLISH NEED TO KNOW

This is such an integral part of PBL. PBL is about inquiry that is led by the students. One of the best ways to begin inquiry is to ask questions. Once students have considered the driving question and have read through the project outline, they will no doubt begin to ask a lot of questions. This is a good thing. Your job is not to answer the questions, but rather to encourage students to record and develop their questions further. You may like to do this as a class group, having students call out their questions and allocating one student the role of scribe. These questions can then be recorded onto the project wall, becoming a guide for students' learning through the project. If you think students need to develop their questioning strategies, you could try using the star-bursting technique. Have students draw a six-pointed star in the middle of a sheet of paper. On each point write: where, what, how, when, why and who. Encourage students to think of as many questions about the project (and its related content) beginning with each word, and record them on the paper. You will be surprised by the richness and diversity of the questions students ask. This lesson also provides an opportunity for students to begin thinking about the audience for their presentation and product. For example: Who will it be? What are their interests? How do we cater for these interests? Note that all of these questions will stem from the original driving question, and this means that you must have a strong driving question that has the potential to generate further questions and set the stage for students' inquiry. Below is an example.

SET UP TEAMS

This is a fairly quick step in PBL, but it can be very difficult for students. Most students will initially resent being "forced" to work with peers with whom they don't usually socialise. This is normal. Our experience is that after the first few projects, students become much more accustomed to working with a range of peers, and even begin to acknowledge the strengths of others with whom they may not usually work. As a teacher, you need to think about what the benefits will be to having students working in teams for a specific project. The obvious reason is that we want to develop teamwork skills such as collaboration, communication and collective decision-making; however, other valid reasons include appreciating diversity in learning styles and deepening understanding by considering a range of perspectives on an issue. When teams are first established, it is a good idea to encourage students to choose a team name – this gives them a collective identity. Try to remember the team names and refer to each team by their name at some point during each lesson. We also find it handy to run a team-building activity. One such activity could be devising a team contract where, as a team, students commit to certain expected behaviours such as being on time to class, not interrupting when someone else is talking or putting in their personal best each lesson. You might like to provide your students with a scaffold for this, and we've provided you with an example in the "Part Three: Additional Resources" section of this book. Routine is very important to PBL, so encourage students to select someone in the team to be responsible for collecting the team's project packet each lesson and one member to be the team spokesperson for when they need to share ideas with the teacher or class.

CREATE A PROJECT CALENDAR

A project calendar is designed to keep students forward-focused. PBL is a student-directed methodology where students are required to take responsibility for their own learning. As such, a project calendar can help students keep themselves organised and ensure that they are working towards clearly established deadlines. These deadlines should be negotiated with the teacher as a whole class; however, there will be times when individual teams will have different deadlines to ensure that learning is differentiated effectively. We recommend that a project calendar includes clearly identified dates for formative assessment – that is, assessment of learning through strategies like plans, drafts, mini-presentations, quizzes and meetings with team leaders. This project has students completing two products – a video game review and a persuasive speech. The project calendar must reflect opportunities for teams to receive feedback on these products at the process stage. Students will also negotiate with the teacher opportunities for direct instruction – this is where the teacher runs a traditional, teacher-centred lesson – and time to receive and apply feedback. For this project, students are required to review a video game, and therefore a number of lessons will need to be dedicated to whole-class instruction on textual analysis of this form. See the calendar on the next page.

PROJECT CALENDAR

PROJECT: GAME 2 LEARN
DATES:

	MONDAY	TUESDAY	WEDNESDAY	THURSDAY	FRIDAY
PROJECT WEEK ONE					
	Hook lesson	Project intro – project outline, KWL table, Need to Know list	Discover – star-bursting	Discover – research video games in education	Discover – research video games in education
PROJECT WEEK TWO					
	Discover – video game analysis	Discover – video game analysis	Discover – features of review and speech	Create – review	Create – review
PROJECT WEEK THREE					
	Create – review	Create – speech	Create – speech	Create – speech	Create – speech
PROJECT WEEK FOUR					
	Share – practise speech	Share – practice speesh	Share – prep for event	Share – event	Reflect

 REPRODUCIBLE – PART TWO: SAMPLE PROJECTS YEAR 7 – 1. GAME 2 LEARN

DISCOVER

GETTING TO KNOW VIDEO GAMES AND PERSUASIVE TEXTS

This project has an extended "inquiry" phase because students must conduct research into the use of video games for learning, as well as discover the structure and language features of a review and a speech. Of course, how you decide to get your students to engage with the video games is up to you and highly dependent on your students. Some teachers will want their students to engage with the video game form through a whole-class deconstruction of a game. Some teachers will read published game reviews. Other teachers may have their students play a wide range of video games – on phones, tablets, consoles and PCs – and review them using a given checklist of features. Ultimately, students are required to discover the pros and cons of using video games in the classroom, the design elements of video games, and the language and structure of persuasive texts through a process of inquiry, whether that is guided or independent.

GETTING TO KNOW THE STRUCTURE AND LANGUAGE OF A SPEECH

At some point your students will have identified that they need to know how to write and deliver a speech. This provides them with an opportunity to "book in" the teacher to deliver a whole-class lesson of some description. This may be a lively class discussion, a series of collaborative activities or providing students with written information about speeches. When supporting students with their discovery of a new type of text, it is important to spend time looking at the language features specific to this type of text, as well as the spelling, punctuation and grammar that students will likely need support with. While it is highly likely that you will identify common weaknesses in these basics when you're reading initial drafts, it is still a good idea to "front-load" by addressing likely errors before they occur.

FORMATIVE ASSESSMENT 1

During the above inquiry, it is essential that you take frequent opportunities to check for understanding. There are many formative assessment strategies that can be used to check for understanding, however, some are more suited to this project than others. The following formative assessment strategies should be used during the inquiry stage of the project to help you assess for students' understanding:

- multiple-choice quizzes on the persuasive devices and/or video game elements
- exit slips asking students to summarise their main points for or against video games being used for learning
- matching activity where students match a persuasive device with its definition
- give each team one or two of the Need to Know questions from the project wall and have them try to answer them, sharing their answers with the class.

If you discover that there is a gap in students' knowledge or understanding, then take the time to address this as well as you can. If it is a problem shared by the class, address it as a whole class. If it is a problem shared by a few students, bring them together in a small team and chat with them about ways to address the issue. This can be done while the rest of the class is working on an activity individually or in their project teams.

CREATE 🎵

This part of the project should take approximately half of the time allocated for the project. Students will spend time planning and drafting their review and their presentation. The handout on the next page will help students with planning their review. Once each student has written a draft, time should be given for peer feedback using the peer-feedback checklist. For best practice regarding the use of this checklist, read the information in "Part One: A Word About PBL and Assessment". Once students have given and received peer feedback, they should spend some time refining their review based on the suggestions of their peers and their teacher, if time permits. Final video game reviews can be posted online to share with a wider audience.

Now that students have a solid appreciation of the video game form and persuasive texts, they will begin working in teams on their speech. It is a good idea to try to find a space larger than the classroom, such as the drama room, the school hall or the school oval. This will give students the freedom to experiment with their speeches without feeling shy or embarrassed. On the following pages, there is a brief handout that will support your students through the scripting and rehearsal of their speech. Formative assessment continues throughout this process, as you now have the opportunity to spend time with each team and help with their speeches. You might like to use the "Draft Speech Checklist" to give students formative feedback at this stage.

REVIEW FEEDBACK

NAME:		TEACHER ASSESSMENT:	
	CRITERIA	YES	NO
1	Does the review persuade the reader to agree with the reviewer's opinion?		
2	Does the review provide evidence to support the ideas being discussed in each paragraph?		
3	Are a wide variety of persuasive devices (e.g. rhetorical questions, repetition, strong verbs and adverbs) used to enhance the reviewer's opinion?		
4	Is vocabulary varied, interesting and relevant to the video game being reviewed?		
5	Are all the sentences well structured and do they make sense?		
6	Is all the punctuation correct?		
7	Are all the words spelled correctly?		
8	Does the review include the correct structure including introduction, body and conclusion?		
9	Are connectives (e.g. also, similarity, furthermore) used effectively to show transitions between paragraphs?		
10	Have paragraphs been used correctly to help the reader follow the reviewer's argument?		

Medals: (main strengths of this review)

Missions: (improvements needed for your next review)

REPRODUCIBLE – PART TWO: SAMPLE PROJECTS YEAR 7 – 1. GAME 2 LEARN

SPEECH: STEPS TO SUCCESS

Public speaking can be daunting if you don't prepare, so it's important to take some time to break this task down into small, manageable chunks. The table below gives you a chance to see each part of the process involved in presenting a great speech. Using this table as your guide, you will be able to better plan to achieve each part bit by bit. It makes sense, really, since when you have a clear goal of what you need to do, you are more likely to do a task better. What's better is that you get to reward yourself along the way!

CHUNKS: STEPS REQUIRED TO ACHIEVE YOUR PERSONAL BEST	TIME REQUIRED FOR THIS TASK:	COMPLETE STEP BY:	☐ WHEN DONE
Check the question and make sure that you understand the task/question	15 mins		
Use the star-bursting strategy to identify your main inquiry questions	30 mins		
Once you have decided on your inquiry questions, it's time to research to find your answers (e.g. books in the library, talk to friends or family, or search the internet)	30 mins		
Spend time reading the resources you have collected. Highlight the important parts and decide on your position on the topic	20 mins		
Organise information in order of importance for your speech topic	10 mins		
Make sure you understand the correct structure of a speech	5 mins		
Add flesh to the bones of your speech skeleton by writing your first draft	20 mins		
Read your draft out loud to TWO critical friends and have them make suggestions for improvement using the draft speech checklist	50 mins		
Write a second draft, adding in any changes necessary	50 mins		
Edit your speech (Are all words spelt correctly? Is your introduction engaging? Have you answered the question? Have you written in paragraphs?) Give yourself a reward for finishing the written speech	25 mins		
Begin to memorise your opening. Jot down one dot point or draw an image or symbol that will help you to remember this paragraph. Give yourself a reward for remembering this paragraph	15 mins		
Repeat the previous step with your remaining paragraphs	15 mins		
Practise your speech in front of the bathroom mirror or in front of your friends or family. Try not to use your notes	30 mins		
Reward yourself for successfully completing the assignment	n/a		

 REPRODUCIBLE – PART TWO: SAMPLE PROJECTS YEAR 7 – 1. GAME 2 LEARN

PERSONAL EVALUATION	CIRCLE A NUMBER: 1 = STRONGLY AGREE 5 = DON'T AGREE AT ALL				
I believe that I will have achieved my personal best for this task:	1	2	3	4	5
I believe that I could have tried harder in at least two of the "chunks" above:	1	2	3	4	5
I believe that I could have tried harder in at least three of the "chunks" above:	1	2	3	4	5
I feel that I lacked commitment and because of this I didn't achieve my personal best for this task:	1	2	3	4	5

DRAFT SPEECH CHECKLIST

CRITERIA	NEEDS MORE WORK	OKAY	GOOD
Is the introduction made engaging by using a joke, rhetorical question, strong statement or statistic?			
Does the body have strong paragraphs that give evidence to support ideas?			
Does the speech have a powerful conclusion that ends memorably?			
Are all sentences structured correctly so they make sense and aren't too long?			
Has correct paragraphing, punctuation, spelling and grammar been used?			
Medals: (two things that are great about the speech)			
Missions: (two things that need improving)			

REPRODUCIBLE – PART TWO: SAMPLE PROJECTS YEAR 7 – 1. GAME 2 LEARN

SHARE

You and your students have finally made it to the end of the project. This part of the project will be both stressful and rewarding. Remember that your students are just as anxious at this stage as you are. It is essential that you give your students lots of encouragement and support but don't fall into the trap of doing the work for them. It doesn't matter if their final speech isn't perfect; it simply needs to be a reflection of their learning and effort as a team. At least a week before the final speeches, make sure that you have a good idea about who will be attending and that you have the ideal space booked.

SUMMATIVE ASSESSMENT

Remind students that they will be assessed on their speech as a team or as individuals – whichever you choose – and that you will be using a checklist to give them feedback. It is important that students get a copy of the checklist while they are preparing their speech so they understand the success criteria.

POST-PROJECT REFLECTION/EVALUATION

Reflection on learning is an integral part of PBL. The best type of reflection is highly defined and focused on the specific learning targets for the project. Ensure your reflection questions allow students to reflect on their development of these skills and capacities. This will allow them to draw a connection between what their goals were, what they did and how they grew as learners. There are so many ways that you can get your students to engage in reflection on their learning. You might get them to record a podcast describing their favourite and least favourite experiences during the project. You could get students to sit together in small groups and share three skills they've mastered and three new facts they've learnt. Two students could interview each other and record their reflections for the teacher to read later. We often get our students to blog using the "think, puzzle, explore" visible-thinking strategy. For this project, get your students to reflect on their experience of the project by answering the questions below. You could have them put their answers in their portfolio to keep as a record of their learning, or they could use one of the other strategies mentioned above.

GAME 2 LEARN – END OF PROJECT REFLECTION

1. One of the learning goals for this project was to be able to support an argument with evidence. How well did you achieve this goal?
2. What did you learn about video games during this project that you didn't already know?
3. What is one thing about writing a review and a speech that you found hard at the beginning of the project, but you find easier now?
4. What are the three most important things you learnt during this project?
5. What is something you taught your teacher or classmates during this project?
6. During this project you had to present in front of an audience. Describe the learning process you took from choosing your position on the topic to delivering the final speech.
7. What are six adjectives that best describe this project?

YEAR 7
2. #LOVEOZYA

PROJECT AT A GLANCE:

 **DRIVING QUESTION:** How might reading Australian young adult fiction help teens make positive life decisions?

 DISCOVER: Students study an Australian young adult novel prescribed by the teacher, as well as reading at least one other Australian young adult novel of their own choosing.

 CREATE: Students work in small teams to plan, draft, edit and create a multimodal text that answers the driving question. These texts may include: a YouTube video/vlog, a picture book, podcast, video game, animation or a suite of illustrated poems. Individually students will write a personal essay in response to the project's driving question.

 SHARE: Students will contribute their multimodal text to a #LoveOzYA exhibition at the local shopping centre to encourage teenagers to read more Australian young adult fiction.

TAKE IT FURTHER: Invite other local secondary schools to join the project and contribute to the #LoveOzYA exhibition; invite your local newspaper to report on the campaign; have students publish their finished products to your school's YouTube channel; or collaborate with a local bookshop to enhance your exhibition.

 ASSESSMENT: Students will be assessed individually on an extended response to the driving question, and they will be assessed as a team on the quality of their multimodal text.

 21ST-CENTURY SKILLS: ICT, critical thinking, creative thinking and collaboration.

LITERACY: grammar – sentence types, clauses, connectives; punctuation – semicolons, commas, ellipses, dashes and brackets; reading – summarising, monitoring, visualising, making predictions; paragraphs

TYPE OF TEXT: imaginative (novel), informative/persuasive/imaginative (multimodal text)

LANGUAGE FEATURES OF TEXTS: theme, plot, characterisation, settings, figurative language, film/visual techniques

POSSIBLE TEXTS: *The First Third* by Will Kostakis (2013); *The Bone Sparrow* by Zana Fraillon (2016); *Green Valentine* by Lili Wilkinson (2015); *Laurinda* by Alice Pung (2014); *Freedom Ride* by Sue Lawson (2015); *Begin, End, Begin* edited by Danielle Binks (2017) and *Lockie Leonard, Human Torpedo* by Tim Winton (1990)

How might reading Australian young adult fiction help teens make positive life decisions?

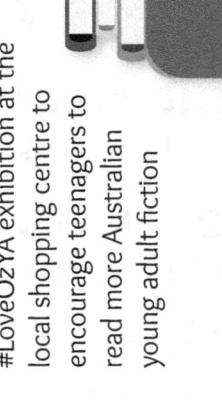

Young people today face a lot of pressures and because of this it can be hard to make the best decisions all of the time. There are many different people and circumstances that can influence the choices we make. The risks we take can be determined by how we think other people will react and the consequences of this for us. During this project, you will be spending some time reading Australian young adult fiction. You will discover the decisions the characters in these stories have to make, and how these decisions impact them – and those around them – in the short and long term.

Discover:

- Young adult fiction novels written by Australian authors
- How authors engage their readers in the world of their novel
- How to communicate your own response to the driving question in the personal essay form

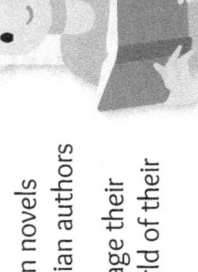

Create:

- A personal essay that answers the driving question
- As part of a small team, plan, draft, edit and create a multimodal text that answers the driving question. These texts may include: a YouTube video or vlog, a picture book, podcast, video game, animation or a suite of illustrated poems

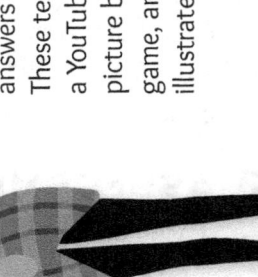

Share:

- Your team's multimodal text with the general public as part of the #LoveOzYA exhibition at the local shopping centre to encourage teenagers to read more Australian young adult fiction

BEFORE YOU BEGIN

CONTACT EXPERTS/ROCK STARS

Young adult fiction is VERY popular today. You would be surprised by how many young people read it for pleasure, and even more surprised by how many share and review their reads in online spaces such as Instagram, YouTube and Tumblr in their spare time. The prevalence of bookstagrammers (people who are devoted to sharing their love of novels via Instagram) and book vloggers (people who are devoted to sharing their love of novels via YouTube) means that it should be relatively easy to get in contact with someone passionate about young adult fiction to connect with your class. You may have ex-students who are bookstagrammers or book vloggers, so it's worth reaching out to that part of your network and asking. Also, the #LoveOzYA movement (which was created by a group of passionate Australian readers, writers and teachers) has a website and regular events that you can tap into at *loveozya.com.au*. It would be ideal if you could organise an Australian young adult fiction writer to come and speak to students just before they begin to plan their multimodal texts and then return for the #LoveOzYA exhibition.

MODIFY PROJECT OUTLINE

Now is the time to modify the given project outline. You may decide to change some of the key elements in order to meet the needs of your students. Look closely at the three stages of learning – Discover, Create, Share – and consider what might need to be modified. Remember that PBL is all about engaging students through making content significant for their needs and interests. You will also need to modify the project outline to indicate due dates for formative and summative assessment.

ORGANISE PROJECT PACKETS

This is a rather large project, as it requires students to engage with two novels, write a personal essay responding to the driving question and then compose a multimodal text. To help keep your students' learning on track and to keep them organised, use your project packets well. There are a number of resources that will be useful to include in these project packets, including:

- Information on structure and language of a personal essay. These resources should match the needs of your students and may take the form of worksheets or links to websites with interactive activities. Some students will require scaffolds to support their writing.
- Information on young adult fiction. As with the above, this may simply take the form of a worksheet students complete using information from their own inquiry, or you may choose to give them specific information. This choice will depend on the skills of your students and your ability to access technology.
- A team contract (you might like to use the template provided in Part 3: Additional Resources).
- A checklist for students' personal essays.
- Mnemonics for text types.
- A project calendar.
- Multimodal texts checklists.
- A copy of the project outline.

PLAN PROJECT TEAMS

This is a project where you might like to "stream" your teams into ability groups. This will allow you to spend more time working closely with the teams of students who require much more support to be successful with the project. We would suggest teams being no bigger than four. This will give each student the opportunity to contribute meaningfully to this project.

CREATE SPACE FOR A PROJECT WALL

Your project wall needs to be highly visible. If you don't have a homeroom, you might like to seek permission from the school executive to use an external space, such as a wall outside the classroom that you use for that class. Another alternative is to have a digital project wall. There are some great web tools to create these, such as Weebly and Glogster. These sites allow you to create interactive project walls, where students can click on the project outline and see it in greater detail, or access additional resources like scaffolds or checklists. Things to include on this project's wall:

- project outline
- project calendar
- key terms
- Need to Know
- the project title
- the project's driving question.

LAUNCH YOUR PROJECT

HOOK LESSON

As with all projects, the hook lesson must be fun and engaging for students and launch inquiry into the project's content. This project provides you with a range of options to engage your students. Here is one suggestion for a fun hook lesson:

- Using a variety of basic materials (such as plastic cups, cardboard boxes, paperclips etc.), design and build an amusement park that represents life as a teenager. For example, "The Big Drop" is about being dumped, and "The Mood Swings" would be a great name for the swing ride. Have students present their model to the class, explaining what each aspect represents.

POSE DRIVING QUESTION

The lesson after the hook lesson is where students are given access to the project's driving question for the first time. This project's driving question is: *How might reading Australian young adult fiction help teens make positive life decisions?*

This is an example of a longer, more complex driving question, however, it relates specifically to students' own lives, and therefore should be engaging due to this significance.

Of course, if you don't like this question, or you think your students won't, you can change it to something more suitable. Once you pose this question to the students, get them to immediately write down their own, unmediated personal response to it. This will become their hypothesis, which will be tested and reshaped as they work through the Discover learning stage.

HAND OUT PROJECT OUTLINE

We recommend that the project outline is printed off in colour or printed onto coloured paper. As soon as you hand the project outline out, have students sit quietly and read through it, using a pen or highlighter to identify any information that they feel they do not understand or that they have questions about. This is an essential step, as this information becomes part of what the class has identified as what they need to know.

ESTABLISH NEED TO KNOW

This is your opportunity to encourage students to share their questions about the project. What you want from your students is for them to begin asking open-ended and critical questions that acknowledge that more learning must occur and that the teacher does not know everything. You can make establishing the Need to Know questions into a game. Have all students write down several questions that they feel they need to know the answers to in order to be successful. Tell them that in order to win this game, the originality and quality of their questions is very important. Ask all students to stand behind their desks. Have each student read out one of their questions. If others have the same question and the student does not have any other original questions, they must sit down. Keep going around the room having students contribute their questions until there is only one person left standing. As the questions are being read out, write the really good ones on the board to create a class list of what they need to know to complete the project successfully.

SET UP TEAMS

Putting students into their teams is usually a noisy activity. A good way to get them to stay quiet is to write the names of the team members on the board and then tell the class that those who find their team members the quickest while remaining silent will get a prize. At this stage, it is a good idea to tell students that they will be working with their teams closely during the Discover stage as critical friends to help write their individual personal essays, and then during the Create stage they will work together to create their multimodal text for the #LoveOzYA exhibition. It is up to you if you wish to draw or deflect attention from the fact that the teams have been chosen based on ability – if this is the strategy you choose for this project.

CREATE A PROJECT CALENDAR

A project calendar is designed to keep students forward-focused. PBL is a student-directed methodology, where students are required to take responsibility for parts of their learning. As such, a project calendar can help students keep themselves organised and ensure that they are working towards clearly established deadlines. Some things to include on the project calendar for this project are:

- due dates for personal essay plan, draft and revised version
- due dates for multimodal text plan, draft and revised version
- date of exhibition.

DISCOVER

The Discover stage for this project is quite teacher-directed, but it is not teacher-centred. Students are actively working through a range of collaborative learning tasks to develop their understanding of the ways in which the Australian young adult fiction they are studying helps teens make positive life decisions. The following is a suggested series of activities you may wish to run with your students at this stage of the project.

Students spend time in class reading aloud or listening to the novel being read aloud. The teacher will introduce the MS J HOTTI narrative devices mnemonic to help students identify devices used by the author to develop characters, plot, settings and themes in the novel.

- Students take notes about the narrative using the Novel Matrix. This can be completed as a whole class if necessary.
- Students may need to be allocated chapters to read for homework. Their understanding of these chapters can be assessed via a quick comprehension quiz at the beginning of the lesson.
- In the last lesson of the week students return to the driving question and write a couple of paragraphs discussing what decisions are made by characters in the novel and evaluating how effective they are. They should also discuss what narrative devices the author has used to present these decisions to the reader. The teacher should model this type of response for students.
- Students do a team deconstruction of an example personal essay (this could be a blog post about a novel) – identifying content and stylistic features. The teacher may wish to give the Personal Essay Checklist to students to use as a guide for their deconstruction.
- Students do a class co-construction of a "Top Ten Features of a Personal Essay".
- Students plan their personal essay – main thesis and lines of argument – and get warm and cool feedback from a critical friend in their team.
- With teacher support where appropriate, students draft their personal essays in response to the driving question, self-assessing along the way with the Personal Essay Checklist.

PROSE TEXTS

M OOD

S YMBOLISM

J UXAPOSITION

H YPERBOLE

O XYMORON

T ONE

T HEME

I MAGERY

I RONY

PERSONAL ESSAY CHECKLIST

NAME:

	CRITERIA	TEACHER/PEER FEEDBACK			I USED FEEDBACK TO IMPROVE ...		
		STILL LEARNING	ACHIEVED	ABOVE & BEYOND	DIDN'T	TRIED	DID
1	Does the essayist establish a personal and distinctive voice throughout the essay?						
2	Are a variety of sentence types used to create pace, mood and focus? Sentence types include simple, compound, complex.						
3	Is interesting, varied and appropriate vocabulary used to help the reader better understand the ideas of the personal essay?						
4	Does the essayist answer the driving question by presenting a personal and thoughtful argument?						
5	Does the introduction hint at the ideas in the body and/or directly engage with the driving question?						
6	Are the language features of an essay used to effectively engage readers? Language features may include emotive language, humour, symbolism, figurative language, juxtaposition, first-person narrative, personal, subjective voice and/or modality.						
7	Does the personal essay have correct grammar, punctuation, spelling and paragraphing?						
8	Do the body paragraphs present thoughtful and personal ideas that relate to the driving question?						
9	Do the body paragraphs provide evidence to support the ideas being discussed in the paragraph?						
10	Does the conclusion of the essay provoke readers' thoughts/emotions/imagination and make them want to continue reading or ask questions of the essayist?						

Medals: (main strengths of this personal essay)

Missions: (improvements needed for this personal essay)

 REPRODUCIBLE – PART TWO: SAMPLE PROJECTS YEAR 7 – 2. #LOVEOZYA

FORMATIVE ASSESSMENT 1

Below are some strategies you might like to use to check students' understanding and skills at this stage of the project.

- Quiz students on the MS J HOTTI mnemonic.
- Give students a comprehension quiz on novel characters, setting, plot and themes.
- Ask students to draft their personal essay.
- Have students complete the "Responding to Prescribed Novel" worksheet under exam-style conditions.
- Have students answer all the Need to Know questions relevant to the Discover stage of the project individually or as a class.

RESPONDING TO PRESCRIBED NOVEL

Base your answers to the questions below on the novel you have studied in class. Remember to pay attention to the types of VERBS used in each question.

1. Identify the main characters and settings in the novel.
   _____
   _____

2. Describe the plot of the novel.
   _____
   _____
   _____
   _____

3. Explain the main theme of the novel.
   _____
   _____
   _____
   _____
   _____

4. Analyse how the author has used the elements of narrative to communicate their main theme.
   _____
   _____
   _____
   _____
   _____
   _____

CREATE ♬

The main product students are creating for this project is their multimodal text. In the Discover stage of the project, students developed their understanding of how Australian young adult fiction helps teens make positive life choices. Now at the Create stage, each team will work together to compose an engaging multimodal text — this can be imaginative, informative or persuasive — that communicates this knowledge to others, with the hopes of encouraging more teens to read Australian young adult fiction. Below is a series of activities you may wish to follow for this stage of the project:

- The teacher reintroduces the project outline, drawing attention to the final Create task. Return to the original KWL table. As a class, consider students' questions in the W column of the KWL table and identify what answers they can give and what they have learnt so far. This information can be added to the L column.

- The class brainstorms methods of communicating how Australian young adult fiction helps teens make positive life choices. Each team will create ONE multimodal text — this should include at least two modes (gestural, spatial, written, audio, visual) and can be print or digital. Teacher shows models of multimodal texts and introduces the mnemonics for other types of texts — LT MC GAVSSS (visual texts), MS SALEM (film) and MR RAP ASSO (poetry).

- Student teams allocate roles and responsibilities, e.g. team leader, note-taker, researcher, creative mind, maker. Teams negotiate their "angle" for their multimodal text — *what do we want to communicate to our audience about Australian young adult fiction and the choices teens often must make* (WHAT)? Once this is established, teams begin planning how they will communicate these ideas to their audience via their multimodal text (HOW). Remind students that each team might focus on different types of life choice teens must make, e.g. decisions relating to bullying, peer pressure, managing schoolwork, getting a job, boyfriends/girlfriends, friendship, dealing with parents, puberty, etc.

- Team leaders present their WHAT and HOW ideas to the teacher, who provides feedback to each leader.

- Teams continue to work on their multimodal texts with ongoing feedback from the teacher, as well as self-assessment using the given checklists.

- The teacher should encourage individual and team goal-setting and end-of-lesson reflection.

POETRY

METAPHOR
RHYTHM

RHYME
ALLITERATION
PERSONIFICATION

ASSONANCE
SIMILE
SYMBOLISM
ONOMATOPOEIA

FILM TEXTS

MOVEMENT

SHOTS

SOUND

ANGLES

LIGHTING

EDITING

MISE EN SCÈNE

VISUAL TEXTS

LINE

TEXTURE

MODALITY

COLOUR

GAZE

ANGLES

VECTORS

SHOTS

SALIENCE

SYMBOLISM

FORMATIVE ASSESSMENT 2

Below are some strategies you might like to use to check students' understanding and skills at this stage of the project.

- Students can use a checklist to give peer feedback on their draft multimodal texts.
- Teams can use the checklists to self-assess their drafts and refine.
- Lead a gallery walk of the WHAT and HOW of multimodal texts.
- Students complete the "project management log" and the teacher checks completion of tasks at the end of each lesson.
- *Thirty-second check-in:* One team member presents a 30-second overview of team's progress. Teams should outline what they have completed and what still needs to be done. They should ask for feedback from their peers.
- *Team-leader meetings*: The teacher meets with all team leaders in a small group to discuss the progress of each team and to deal with any common issues arising. This is a good opportunity for the teacher to target any common problems noticed, such as sloppy presentation or similarities between products.
- *Confession booth*: Each student spends 30 seconds videoing or writing their concerns about their team's progress. Focus is specifically on team members contributing to team goals.
- Each team gives a three- to five-minute presentation of their exhibit. They can use Microsoft PowerPoint or Prezi to support their presentation. They must cover the WHAT and the HOW of their exhibit and present a convincing, personal and original response to the driving question.

PICTURE BOOK FEEDBACK

NAME:							
	GOALS	**PEER ASSESSMENT #1**			**SELF-ASSESSMENT #2**		
		DIDN'T	TRIED	DID	DIDN'T	TRIED	DID
1	Have the authors and illustrators included appropriate information about Australian YA?						
2	Does the picturebook effecively answer the driving question?						
3	Have the authors and illustrators effectively used visual techniques (LT MC GAVSSS) to create characters, mood and ideas?						
4	Is the written text of a high standard without errors in punctuation and spelling?						
5	Is the picture book beautifully presented?						

Medals: (main strengths of this picture book)

Missions: (improvements needed for this picture book)

SUITE OF POEMS FEEDBACK

NAME:							
	GOALS	**PEER ASSESSMENT #1**			**SELF-ASSESSMENT #2**		
		DIDN'T	TRIED	DID	DIDN'T	TRIED	DID
1	Have the poets included appropriate information about Australian YA?						
2	Have the poets used effective and appropriate poetic devices to create visual and aural images?						
3	Are the poems well structured with correct use of lines and stanzas?						
4	Do the poems present an effective answer to the driving question?						
5	Is the work beautifully presented with consideration of fonts, colour etc?						
6	Have appropriate visual elements been used to communicate the poem's themes?						

Medals: (main strengths of this picture book)

Missions: (improvements needed for this picture book)

SHORT FILM FEEDBACK

NAME:

	GOALS	PEER ASSESSMENT #1			SELF-ASSESSMENT #2		
		DIDN'T	TRIED	DID	DIDN'T	TRIED	DID
1	Have the filmmakers included appropriate information about Australian YA?						
2	Does the short film have a strong answer to the driving question?						
3	Have the filmmakers used camera angles and shots effectively to communicate ideas and creat mood?						
4	Have the filmmakers used sound (dialogue, music, SFX) effectively?						
5	Has the short film been edited effectively using cuts, fades, titles etc. where appropriate?						

Medals: (main strengths in this short film)

Missions: (improvements needed for the short film)

PROJECT MANAGEMENT LOG: INDIVIDUAL GUIDE

DRIVING QUESTION:

NAME:

TASK	DATE DUE	STATUS	DONE

This document reproduced with permission from BIE

SHARE

When students have finalised their multimodal texts, devote a lesson to teams sharing the finished products with their peers. This is an enjoyable activity but also helps you see that work is completed to an appropriate standard for display at the exhibition. You can also ask each team member a question about the final product, to ensure all students have contributed.

When planning for the exhibition, write up a "to do" list as a class and allocate students roles and responsibilities. These will include: creating and sending invitations to family and friends for the exhibition launch, designing displays (teams may like to have a 200-word rationale for their multimodal text), liaising with shopping centre management and a local bookshop, organising food and drinks for the exhibition launch, ensuring all digital multimodal texts are accessible via QR codes or some type of screen to view, etc. You may need to go on a class excursion to the venue to organise and set up the exhibition – where appropriate. Organising a launch of the exhibition where some students read excerpts from their personal essay and talk about the project is a nice touch, as is inviting one or two local Australian young adult fiction authors.

POST-PROJECT REFLECTION/EVALUATION

This project, like all projects, requires students to reflect on their learning. This can be done as a class discussion, where you sit together in a circle and talk about what they loved and didn't love about the project. Perhaps you might like to use a Plus-Minus-Interesting (PMI) table to evaluate the project? One has been included on the next page for you to use. This makes the focus on the project itself, which requires you, as the teacher, to be open to criticism. This is hard at first, because having students critique your work is probably an unfamiliar experience. But we've found it to be a very liberating experience, as well as a productive strategy to improve the way we teach. Another important reflection for this project is individual student reflection. Ask them to look back at their personal strengths and weaknesses as a team member that they identified early in the project. It is now time for them to consider each, and reflect on a time where they used their strengths to support their group's learning, and a time when they worked hard to overcome their weaknesses to avoid negatively impacting on learning.

#LOVEOZYA: PROJECT EVALUATION PMI

PLUS	MINUS	INTERESTING

YEAR 7
3. SUSTAINABLE NEWS

PROJECT AT A GLANCE:

 **DRIVING QUESTION:** How can we, as citizen journalists, inform our local community about the importance of sustainable living?

 DISCOVER: Students will engage with a range of news texts to discover the language forms and features of news reports — including those for print, television and radio. Students will research citizen journalism and explore examples of this, as well as researching local sustainability initiatives and issues.

 CREATE: Students will collaborate in small teams to research, draft, edit and publish a news report relating to a local sustainability initiative or issue. These news reports will be published on a class news website called Sustainable News.

 SHARE: Students will plan and run a website launch at a local public institution such as the local library or council.

TAKE IT FURTHER: Connect your English class with a science and/or geography class and make this a cross-curricular project.

 ASSESSMENT: News report

 21ST-CENTURY SKILLS: critical thinking, ICT, collaboration, ethical understanding

LITERACY: *grammar* – pronouns, verbs, active/passive voice, sentence structure; *reading* – summarising, monitoring; *punctuation* – commas, punctuating direct speech

TYPE OF TEXT: informative

LANGUAGE FEATURES OF TEXTS: objective language, register, by-line, paragraphing, headline, direct and indirect quotations, sentence types, modality

POSSIBLE TEXTS: There are many excellent news sites for students: Crinkling, Herald Sun Kid's News and Behind the News are highly recommended. ABC Splash also has excellent resources for helping students learn about writing news reports.

SUSTAINABLE NEWS

March, 2 February 2018

How can we, as citizen journalists, inform our local community about the importance of sustainable living?

Discover:

- What is citizen journalism?
- What are the structure and language features of news reports?
- What are some of the issues and initiatives relating to sustainable living in our local area?

Create:

- Working in a small team, research, draft, edit and publish a news report relating to a local sustainability initiative or issue.
- Publish your news report on our Sustainable News website.

Share:

- Plan and run a launch for the Sustainable News website at a local public institution such as the local library or council.

BEFORE YOU BEGIN

CONTACT EXPERTS

This is an issues-based project. Students will be engaged in meaningful research into issues relating to sustainability within their local area. They will then spend time considering solutions and ways to advocate for the local community to adopt more sustainable lifestyles. Students will also research current initiatives already being implemented as they may choose to report on these to raise greater awareness of the initiative. During the inquiry stage, students should connect with reporters from the local newspaper, as well as individuals working on local sustainability initiatives. This will give authenticity to their inquiry and to the project as a whole. You can also connect with reporters or experts not local to the area by networking with other teachers via social media sites such as Twitter, Facebook and Edmodo. The final presentation is before a public audience. Take some time to get in contact with local stakeholders who have a say in the sustainable living practices of the local community. These may include the mayor, local MPs, not-for-profit organisations, local businesspeople and family members.

HOOK LESSON

The list below has suggestions for hook lessons that could be used to engage students in this project.

- Turn your classroom into a picture gallery by posting a range of images of the impact of human activity on the natural environment to classroom walls or another space. When students enter the room, give them four or five Post-It notes. They are to look at all the images and then select the ones that make them THINK, FEEL or IMAGINE the current and future state of Earth if unsustainable practices continue. Students are to write the appropriate verb at top of the Post-It and then write a sentence explaining what they think, feel or imagine when they look at the image. Songs about the destruction of the environment (such as "License to Kill" by Bob Dylan, "Big Yellow Taxi" by Joni Mitchell, "Don't Go Near the Water" by The Beach Boys and "Monkey's Gone to Heaven" by The Pixies) are played while the students walk silently through the gallery. Remind students of appropriate behaviour for a gallery.

- Give students a range of news articles – some satire or "fake news" and others real news. Have students try to identify which are satire and which are real, and share their reasons for their choices with the class. Good sites for satirical news articles are The Onion, The Shovel and The Chaser.

- Watch a documentary related to sustainable living such as *The War on Waste* series from ABC (2017), or *An Inconvenient Truth* (Davis Guggenheim, 2006).

- Take students for a walk around the outer perimeter of the school and count the number of cars they see, as well as the amount and types of rubbish they see. Return to the class and discuss the impact this might have on the local environment.

DISCOVER

After you have run the hook lesson, handed out the project outline, and established teams and your students' Need to Know questions, the first couple of weeks for this project will have students spending time researching sustainable living issues, initiatives and ideas. Students should be given access to a wide range of quality resources identified by the teacher, rather than just being sent straight to the internet. You may also like to include a novel study to the beginning of this project. Great choices include *Trash* by Andy Mulligan (2010) or *Green Valentine* by Lili Wilkinson (2015). This is a great opportunity to develop students' empathy and to have them think about the ethical decisions faced by others their own age. You may choose to read the novel aloud as a class, or have students read at home and then spend time discussing the novel as a class. This stage of the project will also require students to engage with the language forms and features of news reports, so it is a good idea to spend time reading and deconstructing plenty of examples.

The purpose of the Discover stage is for your students to come away with an appreciation of the range of sustainable living strategies that their local community can begin practising, the language features and structures of news reports, and the role of citizen journalism in our world today.

The following is a list of other possible learning activities for your students at the discovery stage of the project.

- Watch a documentary or series of videos, or listen to podcasts about sustainable living.
- Have students work in small teams researching one of these issues: waste management, local wildlife, local waterways, transportation, energy, air quality or infrastructure.
- Invite a guest speaker in to talk about sustainable living – this could be a science, agriculture or geography teacher from your school. You could also connect with experts online via social media or Skype.
- Teach students how to identify quality sources by introducing them to the CRAAP acronym (Currency, Relevance, Authority, Accuracy, Purpose). This is useful for all types of sources, but especially those found on the internet.
- Show students how to use Cornell Notes, as this will help them avoid inadvertently plagiarising the work of others, and support a deep critical engagement with sources.
- Connect with a class from another country. This could include making a series of videos where each class shares examples of how their community needs to be (or is trying to be) more sustainable. To do this use sites like ePals, Skype in the Classroom, Edmodo or Twitter.
- Conduct an assessment of their own home's impact on the environment, focusing on: energy, water, waste, materials used in construction and design of the home.

FORMATIVE ASSESSMENT 1

Below are some strategies you might like to use to check students' understanding and skills at this stage of the project.

- Give students some comprehension questions on the novel – focusing on theme, plot, characterisation, setting and writing style.
- Give a quiz on the features of a news report.
- Students can submit their Cornell Notes on two sources. The teacher will give formative feedback in the form of "medals" (what they did well) and "missions" (what they need to continue working on).
- Check the quality of the Need to Know questions to assess understanding.
- Use the collaboration rubric in the "Additional Resources" section at the back of this book to check the quality of collaborative behaviours such as sharing ideas, contributing to team discussions and team tasks.

CREATE ♪

In teams, pairs or individually, students will create a news report (for print, television or radio) about sustainable living in the local community. This task gives students much needed voice and choice, as they are given the choice of which news form they will create. Please note that if students choose to create a television or radio report they will need to devote some time at home to complete it. Students are to ground their news report in the research they have conducted about sustainable living in the local community. It is essential that students keep in mind their:

- audience – people attending the website launch, including parents, community members, teachers and politicians
- context – the school is a local institution; therefore students need to think carefully about how they present possibly controversial issues
- purpose – to raise awareness of the need for the local community to embrace new sustainable living practices, and to support existing community sustainability initiatives.

NOTE: As the news reports will be shared on a website, you will need to ask for a student to volunteer to create and curate this website. Another alternative is to ask a senior student to create the website, or to create it yourself. But having a student from your class adopt this role does give more ownership over the work.

FORMATIVE ASSESSMENT 2

Below are some strategies you might like to use to check students' understanding and skills at this stage of the project.

- A peer and/or self-assessment of draft news reports using the given checklists on the following pages.
- A gallery walk for plans of news reports. A gallery walk is where student work (usually drafts or plans) is set out around the room, and the class quietly walks around giving feedback with Post-It notes. We like to have students use the "star, star, wish" strategy, where students give two "stars" for elements of the plan or draft that the they think are great, and their "wish" is what they would like to see improved.

NEWSPAPER ARTICLE GOALS	TEACHER/PEER ASSESSMENT			I USED FEEDBACK TO IMPROVE …		
	DIDN'T	TRIED	DID	DIDN'T	TRIED	DID
Does the headline communicate the main idea of the story?						
Does the article include a by-line?						
Does the article include the date and place?						
Does the lead paragraph catch the reader's attention and make the reader want to keep on reading?						
Does the first paragraph following the lead give the most important information: who, what, where, when, why, how?						
Has the journalist included at least two pertinent quotations from sources?						
Is the article at least 250 words long?						
Has the journalist used correct punctuation, spelling and grammar?						
Do included images or graphs support the ideas in the article?						
MEDALS: (main strengths of this news report)						
MISSIONS: (improvements needed for this news report)						

REPRODUCIBLE – PART TWO: SAMPLE PROJECTS YEAR 7 – 3. SUSTAINABLE NEWS

TELEVISION NEWS REPORT

GOALS	TEACHER/PEER ASSESSMENT			I USED FEEDBACK TO IMPROVE ...		
	DIDN'T	TRIED	DID	DIDN'T	TRIED	DID
Does the host clearly and quickly establish the focus of the report to gain viewer attention?						
Are the main points about the story clearly stated and explained?						
Is the structure logical, smooth and well-organised?						
Does the video include well-selected and well-placed images and text?						
Does the report following the lead give the most important information: who, what, where, when, why, how?						
Has the journalist included at least two pertinent quotations from sources?						
Is the presentation style of the host clear, concise and interesting?						
Is the video between 1–2 minutes long?						
Is the video well-crafted, creative and of a high quality?						

MEDALS: (main strengths of this news report)

MISSIONS: (improvements needed for this news report)

RADIO NEWS REPORT

GOALS	TEACHER/PEER ASSESSMENT			I USED FEEDBACK TO IMPROVE ...		
	DIDN'T	TRIED	DID	DIDN'T	TRIED	DID
Does the host clearly and quickly establish the focus of the report to gain listener attention?						
Are the main points about the story clearly stated and explained?						
Is the structure logical, smooth and well-organised?						
Does the recording include well-selected and well-placed music, sound effects and quotes from interviewees?						
Does the report following the lead give the most important information: who, what, where, when, why and how?						
Has the journalist included at least two pertinent quotations from sources?						
Is the presentation style of the host clear, concise and interesting?						
Is the recording between 1–2 minutes long?						
Is the recording well-crafted, creative and of a high quality?						

MEDALS: (main strengths of this news report)

MISSIONS: (improvements needed for this news report)

REPRODUCIBLE – PART TWO: SAMPLE PROJECTS YEAR 7 – 3. SUSTAINABLE NEWS

SHARE

The dream with this project is that students will see themselves as active agents in their world, as well as appreciating the ways in which the general public can adopt the role of citizen journalists to raise awareness of important local issues. At the final presentation, encourage your students to focus on:

- the need to better promote existing resources and programs to support the embracing of sustainable living practices within the local community
- the importance of young people having a voice on issues relating to the local community and environment, especially through involvement in the news media
- the need to champion the achievements of people successful in changing their lifestyle behaviour to contribute to a better environment and future.

As a class, the students will need to plan a presentation that launches their website – this will need to be informative and persuasive. This presentation needs to appeal to the audience and be powerful enough to effect real change in their world.

To prepare for this stage of the project, students will need to do the following:

- organise a display of their news reports in the venue the day before
- check that videos run on laptops or tablets (for students who have created television and radio reports)
- call and check that special guests know the time and venue for the event – this should be done at least a week before the website launch
- presenters will need to write and rehearse their speeches
- make a list of who is bringing a plate of food or drinks for refreshments to the event.

FORMATIVE ASSESSMENT

Below are some strategies you might like to use to check students' understanding and skills at this stage of the project.

- Thirty-second share: randomly select up to five students to share their learning for that lesson in a 30-second summary.
- Run a rehearsal of the presentation students will give to ensure everyone feels confident. You might like to have a trial question-and-answer session to prepare students for being asked questions about their news reports.

YEAR 7
4. READING REIMAGINED

PROJECT AT A GLANCE:

 **DRIVING QUESTION:** How can technology be harnessed to enhance the reading experiences of teens?

 DISCOVER: Students will research current reading rates and habits of Australian teens and the history of the book, as well as current and emerging technologies impacting how we read.

 CREATE: Students work in small teams to design an innovation to revolutionise how teens read.

 SHARE: In teams, students pitch their design idea in a *Shark Tank* style to a panel of potential "investors".

 ASSESSMENT: A written proposal and pitch.

 21ST-CENTURY SKILLS: critical thinking, creative thinking, ICT, ethical understanding

LITERACY: *grammar* – first person and collective pronouns, verbs, active voice, adjectives, adverbs, sentence structure; *reading* – summarising, monitoring, making connections; *punctuation* – ellipses, semicolons

TYPE OF TEXT: persuasive (pitch)

LANGUAGE FEATURES OF TEXTS: rhetorical devices – rhetorical questions, anaphora, asyndeton, rule of three, anecdote, analogy

POSSIBLE TEXTS: *Inanimate Alice* (2005), *The Boat* interactive graphic novel by Nam Le and adapted by Matt Huynh, The Museum of Mario, The Grey Tales http://thegreytales.net/en/.

HOW CAN TECHNOLOGY BE HARNESSED TO ENHANCE THE READING EXPERIENCES OF TEENS?

The 21st century is a time of rapid innovation and change. So, what impact does this have on the humble book? With more and more teenagers accessing digital technologies like smartphones, laptops, video games and virtual reality for entertainment, reading a book doesn't seem as attractive. Are books too uncool and boring for teenagers today? We know being literate is super important for a successful life, and that reading fiction develops empathy and a deeper appreciation of the world. So how can we encourage teenagers to continue to value reading?

THAT'S YOUR CHALLENGE!

1. BEGIN TO INQUIRE ...
- What is the history of reading?
- What are some historic and contemporary reading innovations?
- What types of texts appeal to teenagers?
- What else do we need to know?

2. THINK LIKE A TEAM OF DESIGNERS ...
- Ideate: generate as many ideas as possible
- Prototype: create multiple drafts of ideas and seek feedback
- Choose: select the best idea
- Refine: use feedback to make your selected idea even better and ready to share.

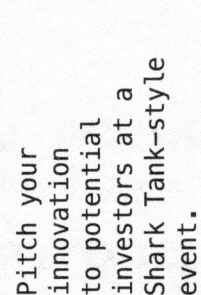

3. PITCH YOUR INNOVATION ...
- Write up your team's proposal for a new type of text for teenagers.
- Prepare a seven- to ten-minute presentation of your ideas.
- Pitch your innovation to potential investors at a Shark Tank-style event.

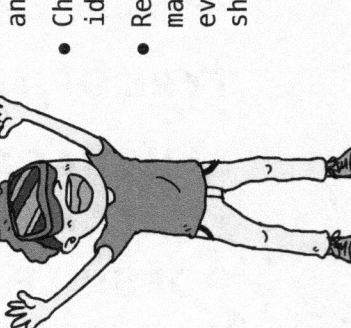

REPRODUCIBLE – PART TWO: SAMPLE PROJECTS YEAR 7 – 4. READING REIMAGINED

BEFORE YOU BEGIN

CONTACT EXPERTS

For this project you may wish to involve content experts or form experts. The content of this project is, mostly, related to reading and engagement. In relation to this aspect of the project you may wish to involve ex-students currently studying literature or education at university or an academic or expert in these fields. Another element is the concept of innovation. You may wish to involve an entrepreneur or designer to talk to students about the design process. For this project you will need to contact and ask the experts to be involved as panellists, who will adopt the role of "investors" to whom the students will pitch their ideas.

PLAN THE HOOK LESSON

For this project, a hook lesson involving reading is essential. Below are some possible ways to hook your students' interest in this project.

- Organise the classroom like a preschool reading corner where students sit on the floor on cushions or a mat, and have a number of popular children's picture books or "big books" read to them. To add to this, provide students with small cartons of milk and plates of biscuits.
- Provide students with a range of creative contemporary fiction that is playful with the reader's experience, such as the Illuminae series by Amie Kaufman and Jay Kristoff (2015). Have students flick through the novel and discuss with a partner how the authors have created a new type of reading experience through its epistolary form and creative use of images and typography.
- Read the class *The Book with No Pictures* by B. J. Novak (2014) and discuss as a group why it is such an engaging book for children.
- Create cardboard Google glasses and have students engage with purpose-built educational apps such as Wizard Academy VR, Google Arts & Culture, and Titans of Space VR.

DISCOVER

After the hook lesson, handing out the project outline, establishing teams and your Need to Know questions (using the KWL table on page 71), this stage of the project will include both teacher-directed and student-directed learning. Looking at the project outline, it is clear to see that there are many aspects to the inquiry for this project. How much support and direction you give students in their inquiry is dependent on the skill level of your students. Here is a quick overview of what students will need to discover at this stage of the project:

- The history of books – there is a great Wikipedia entry on this **https://en.wikipedia.org/wiki/History_of_books** – and how innovations in books have led to changes in reading culture over the years. You could put students in teams to investigate the contributions of different eras or cultures to contemporary reading practices.
- The reading rates among young Australians, including the types of books young Australians read, and the ways in which they access reading materials. Students could look at the impact on access to books given socio-economic and/or cultural barriers.
- The impact that technology has and is having on the way in which young people read – be it fiction or nonfiction. Try to encourage students to focus on fiction and the novel as a form, considering how technology has changed teens' engagement with the novel form. This might include research into book-based social networks, e.g. bookstagrammers and book vloggers.

- The language and structure of a pitch – focusing on rhetorical devices. A good activity is to watch YouTube videos of pitches and have students deconstruct these to identify the criteria for the perfect pitch.

Teachers can assist students in their discovery in the following ways:
- Invite a guest expert to speak to the students about contemporary literature; perhaps someone from a local university or even a bookshop.
- Have students engage with a range of interactive texts (Twine is a good place to find these, as well as text-based video games which can be found on Steam) and virtual reality experiences to help inspire their own innovations.
- Run a series of teacher-led lessons deconstructing *Inanimate Alice* as an example of a contemporary, interactive reading experience. After the first couple of teacher-led lessons, allow students to interact with the last couple of episodes and keep a journal reflecting on how this narrative is reimagining how we read.

FORMATIVE ASSESSMENT 1

Below are some strategies you might like to use to check students' understanding and skills at this stage of the project.

- Have students write a one-page report on the history of the book based on their research.
- Have students create a 10-slide presentation using Google Slides, sharing what they know about current reading trends among Australian teens.
- Give a quiz on *Inanimate Alice* or other interactive fiction your students have engaged with – this could be done quickly using a game of Kahoot.
- Check student's journal entries based on *Inanimate Alice* or other interactive fiction.
- Give a quiz on the structure and language features of a pitch.

KWL

How can technology be harnessed to enhance the reading experiences of teens?

WHAT I KNOW …	WHAT I WONDER …	WHAT I LEARNT …

CREATE 🎵

Before students move into creating their prototype, it is important to get them to re-engage with the driving question to ensure they are focused on the identified problem. There are a number of collaborative-learning and critical-thinking strategies you can use to get students to develop their ideas about the driving question. You may wish to use some of these: think/pair/share, star-bursting, hexagonal thinking, lotus diagrams, hot potato, jigsaws or Venn diagrams.

The Create stage of this project is very similar to the Design Thinking process. Design Thinking is a methodology that allows designers to solve complex problems to meet the identified needs of a specific client. The process involves specific steps: empathise, define, ideate, prototype, test. The first two stages of this process have occurred at the Discover stage of this project, so in the Create stage we move directly to the process of ideation. Ideation is a fun activity wherein students are encouraged to think of many different possible solutions or ideas for the given problem or product. This is often called divergent thinking, and there are a number of strategies that can be used to help students, such as the magic wish (where students write all of the things they wish their product could do – the crazier the better), worst idea ever (where students generate a long list of silly solutions, and then work out how they could make some of them work), snowballing (where each student takes turns in a circle to identify one feature of the product, being sure to add logically to the feature outlined by the speaker before them) and then there are the well-known acronyms SCAMPER and SCUMPS (see the handout on the following pages).

From this diverse range of ideas (from their divergent thinking), students must select up to three of the best ideas to prototype. The prototype stage will be much more basic than that of a working designer's due to resource limitations. It could involve students sketching their innovation with some annotations, or making cardboard or limited digital prototypes. Students should seek feedback, and then select the best idea from their three prototypes – now they are using convergent thinking to identify their best possible solution to the problem. Time in class should then be devoted to refining the selected design for their reading innovation, and preparing it for their pitch.

To support students with the design process, use the handout on the following pages to encourage thoughtful documentation. This will also help them with preparing for their pitch.

FORMATIVE ASSESSMENT 2

Below are some strategies you might like to use to check students' understanding and skills at this stage of the project.

- Check individual or team management log to ensure all students are on task.
- Hand out exit slips using medals and missions – students give themselves up to two medals for things they did well that lesson, and up to two missions for things they need to complete or improve on in the next lesson.
- Check students' understanding of the Create stage by having them write a list of three learning goals they have for this stage of the project.
- Read through students' divergent thinking records (SCUMPS, SCAMPER etc.).
- Assess students' creative thinking using the rubric at the back of this book.

SCAMPER OR SCUMPS FOR CREATIVE IDEAS

SCAMPER IS A MNEMONIC THAT STANDS FOR:

Substitute
E.g. What materials or resources can you substitute or swap to improve books?

Combine
E.g. What would happen if you combined books with another product (like an iPod), to create something new?

Adapt
E.g. What other contexts could you put books into?

Modify
E.g. How could you change the shape, look or feel of books?

Put to another use
E.g. How would books behave differently in another setting?

Eliminate
E.g. How could you make books smaller, faster, lighter or more fun?

Reverse
E.g. What components could you substitute to change the order of a book?

 REPRODUCIBLE – PART TWO: SAMPLE PROJECTS YEAR 7 – 4. READING REIMAGINED

SCUMPS IS A MNEMONIC THAT STANDS FOR:

Size:
How big is it? How big or small could it be?

Colour:
What colour is it produced in? What colours could it be produced in?

Uses:
Who uses the design and for what purpose? Can these uses be added to?

Materials:
What materials are used to manufacture the design and why are these materials used? What other materials could be used?

Parts:
What are the main parts of the design?

Shape:
What shape is the design and why is it that shape? Could it be changed?

PREPARING YOUR PITCH

DOCUMENT THE DESIGN PROCESS

Explain the work you and your team did at each stage of the design process outline below.

IDEATING:

PROTOTYPE:

CHOOSE:

REFINE:

What is the name of the design that you have chosen?

Why did you select this design over your other prototypes?

PREPARING YOUR PITCH - DOCUMENT THE DESIGN PROCESS - CONTINUED

How will your readers access this type of text?

Why have you chosen this method of accessing the text? Think about your audience (other teenagers).

Describe your text in detail. In your description make sure you outline FOUR main features of the text and explain how each one will appeal to teenagers.

FEATURE ONE:

FEATURE TWO:

FEATURE THREE:

PREPARING YOUR PITCH - DOCUMENT THE DESIGN PROCESS - CONTINUED

FEATURE FOUR:

What types of stories will the text feature? Why? You might consider action, adventure, romance, drama, horror, etc.

How much do you expect your readers would pay to read your text? How did you come up with this figure? Make sure you consider how much it would cost to manufacture the text.

How will your innovative text turn teenagers on to reading?

SHARE

Students will work in critical friend teams to plan, draft and edit their pitch. Encourage teams to read each other's plans and drafts and to give constructive feedback using the "praise, inform, praise" or "star, star, wish" feedback method. This will allow students to give both positive and constructive feedback.

The share stage of this project involves students competing with other teams to get the panel of "investors" (invited experts such as authors, innovators, futurists, entrepreneurs and academics specialising in literature). As a class, watch an episode of *Shark Tank* or *Dragon's Den* so students understand the premise of this type of product pitch.

FORMATIVE ASSESSMENT 3

Below are some strategies you might like to use to check students' understanding and skills at this stage of the project.

- Use a "pitch" checklist or rubric for teacher or peer feedback on pitch scripts.
- Have teams present a practice pitch to the class and give feedback using the "star, star, wish" method.
- Have students use the presentation rubric at the back of this book for self-assessment.

YEAR 7
5. ACTING UP

PROJECT AT A GLANCE:

**DRIVING QUESTION:** Why do we tell stories?

DISCOVER: Students learn about the language forms and features of drama by studying a range of traditional and contemporary texts. Students also discover the issues and lessons relevant to Foundation Year students.

CREATE: Working in small teams, students play-build, script and rehearse a three- to five-minute play that communicates an important moral for Foundation Year students.

SHARE: Each team performs their play for an audience of Foundation Year students from a local primary school.

TAKE IT FURTHER: Filmed performances can be posted to the faculty or school YouTube channel, or the primary school's website.

ASSESSMENT: Play script and performance

21ST-CENTURY SKILLS: intercultural understanding, ethical understanding, creative thinking, collaboration and communication

LITERACY: *grammar* – pronouns, verbs, prepositions, qualifiers, interjection, clauses; *reading* – summarising, visualising, predicting, making connections; *punctuation* – parentheses, colons

TYPE OF TEXT: imaginative (play script)

LANGUAGE FEATURES OF TEXTS: dramatic devices – aside, monologue, duologue, stage directions; language features – figurative language, tone, colloquial language, register; five elements of narrative – plot, characterisation, setting, theme, style

POSSIBLE TEXTS: Students should study a range of traditional stories, including Dreaming stories (such as those on Dust Echoes found via ABC Splash) and Greek myths. Students should also study a least one contemporary play such as *Spitting Chips* by Peta Murray (1995), *Two Weeks with the Queen (The Play)* or *Blabbermouth (The Play)* by Mary Morris (1992 and 1996).

BEFORE YOU BEGIN

CONTACT EXPERTS

This project requires students to plan, draft, rehearse and then perform a three- to five-minute morality play before an audience of primary school students. This will require a lot of initial planning. While it is important to allow students to organise the event itself – such as booking a venue, organising the catering and creating invitations – you will need to take responsibility for connecting with a local school and organising to connect your classes.

You may wish to invite a guest expert (such as an actor, playwright, director or academic specialising in children's theatre or literature) to speak with your students at the initial research stage, and invite them back for the final performance. You may choose to have one expert come at the beginning of the project (perhaps an academic) and another come for the final performance (perhaps a local playwright).

PLAN THE HOOK LESSON

The hook lesson for this project can focus on two main aspects of the project: the content (issues and lessons relevant to Foundation Year students) or the form (oral storytelling and drama). The list below has suggestions for hook lessons that could be used to engage students in this project.

- Watch children's theatre on YouTube.
- Invite a local theatre group to perform short, children's theatre-style skits.
- Have students perform or do dramatic readings of funny scripted skits (there are lots to be found online).
- Have students work in small teams to improvise a skit based on a given storyline (e.g. a boy's pet beetle is squashed by his father, or a girl's sister cut all the hair off her favourite doll.)

DISCOVER

The discover stage of learning will see your students engaging closely with a range of oral stories and drama texts. You may choose to engage with the oral stories and drama texts as a whole class (such as with a longer text like Mary Morris' adaptation of Morris Gleitzman's *Two Weeks with the Queen*), or give each team time to discuss, analyse and evaluate a shorter text (such as one of the *Dust Echo* stories, or a Greek myth) and present their learning to the class. We recommend a combination of the two. Firstly, model how to engage critically with oral stories and/or drama texts through a whole-class discussion and co-construction of an analytical paragraph, evaluating the text's strength and weaknesses. In this instance, focus on the use of language and dramatic devices and performance techniques such as pitch, pace, pause, tone, inflection, facial expressions, gestures and body language (use excerpts of filmed productions as examples). Next, allocate each team a shorter text (try to choose texts that have a range of morals, as your students will be constructing a dramatic text that has a moral appropriate for Foundation Year students) and have them complete a similar analysis which they then present for the class. Encourage them to use ICT to support their presentation – this technology might include Microsoft PowerPoint, PowToon or Prezi. You might like to give students the "Analysis of a Play" worksheet on the next page to support their analysis of the text. A one-page worksheet with activities for students to complete in this Discover stage has been included if you feel your students require more structure.

FORMATIVE ASSESSMENT 1

There are a number of different formative assessment strategies that you may choose to use to check students' understanding of the structure and language features of oral stories and drama texts. Below is a list of strategies that you may choose to use.

- A dramatic devices quiz. This should be quick and presented in a non-threatening manner. Ensure students have time to prepare for the quiz because it can cause anxiety in some students to be given a quiz without warning.
- Daily exit slips. For this stage of the project, you might wish to focus on content such as identifying specific dramatic devices or answering two or three questions about a text being studied.
- Think, puzzle and explore blog posts. This could be a homework activity where students write a 100- to 200-word blog post, identifying something that the texts studied that made them think about something new, that puzzled them or was something they would like to explore further.
- Writing an analytical paragraph about an oral story or drama text. This writing task should be modelled and scaffolded to support students. Look at students' work to identify weaknesses that need to be addressed through further inquiry or teacher support.
- A KWL table. As with all projects, the initial stage sees students identify their learning needs through writing Need to Know questions. Looking through these will help you to determine which students will need greater support during the project.

LESSONS FOR THE LITTLE ONES

What lessons do little children need to learn in their first year of school?

Think back to what it was like when you were five or six years old and had just started Foundation Year. What were some of the lessons you had to learn? Think about things like playing outside, making friends, what to eat, how to keep yourself clean and healthy, and doing the right thing in class.

TAKE IT FURTHER

Use the star-bursting technique to generate a list of questions to ask a Foundation Year teacher or a parent of a Foundation Year-aged child. Make sure that your questions relate to the lessons little children need to learn in their first year of school, as this lesson will become the moral to your team's play.

ACTING UP! INQUIRY ACTIVITIES

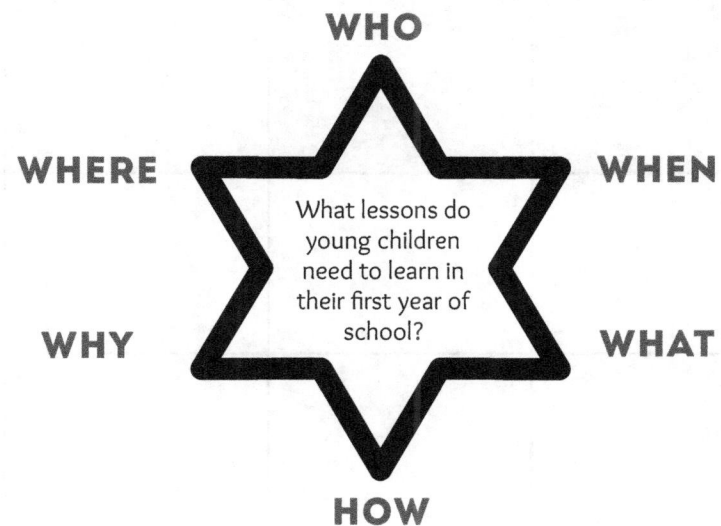

ORAL STORY OR DRAMA TEXT – ANALYSIS:

Read the text you are given by your teacher, and then complete the following four tasks as a team:

1. Identify WHAT the moral of the story is. (One sentence.)

2. Explain HOW the storyteller tries to communicate this message. (Two dramatic/language techniques and an example for each – four sentences.)

3. Evaluate how EFFECTIVELY each technique helps to communicate the storyteller's moral. Think about what the storyteller wants their audience to think/feel/imagine. (Two sentences – one for each dramatic/language technique identified above.)

4. Judge the RELEVANCE of this moral to humanity – why should we care about it? (One to two sentences.)

RESPONDING TO A MORALITY TALE

CONTEXT: make some notes about the times, values and concerns of the storyteller and how they are evident in the text's themes or style.

PURPOSE: What is the purpose of the text?

ISSUES AND CONCERNS: State what the issues or concerns are and discuss how these reflect the times or context of the storyteller.

TONE: Describe the tone. Are there any shifts in tone? What words/phrases help to convey the tone?

LANGUAGE FEATURES: Identify them, comment on their impact on the reader/listener and why the storyteller uses them.

YOUR PERSONAL RESPONSE: Do you agree or disagree with what is being said and do you feel that the storyteller effectively conveys their message?

ANALYSIS OF A PLAY

WHAT IDEAS IS THE PLAY EXPRESSING?	WHAT DRAMATIC OR LANGUAGE DEVICE IS BEING USED TO SAY THIS?	WHAT IS AN EXAMPLE OF THIS DEVICE BEING USED?	WHAT DOES THIS DEVICE MAKE YOU THINK, FEEL OR IMAGINE RELATING TO THE IDEAS OF THE PLAY?	WHY IS THIS IDEA IMPORTANT TO PEOPLE IN THE WORLD? RESTATE THE MAIN IDEA OF THE PLAY.

CREATE 🎵

In this project students will be discovering ideas relating to a specific lesson or moral of their choosing, as well as the structure and language features of play. Students will also be developing their performance skills. This can be quite daunting for some students, so make sure you create a supportive, non-threatening learning environment for your students so they feel confident to take risks and try something new.

PLAY-BUILDING

Each team must select a specific lesson or moral to focus on for their three- to five-minute play. Encourage students to brainstorm a range of possible lessons for their play (we suggest at least 10), and then have them work through a process of elimination where they end up with three ideas they agree are worth pursuing. For each lesson, they should brainstorm possible storylines for their play that could explore each moral — this only needs to be quite rough. They might like to use improvisation to generate some ideas. Once these rough ideas are developed, the team can then vote on the best idea or ask for teacher help in choosing. You can also have teams pair up to share and select the best idea of the three. From this idea and storyline selection, students will collaborate on their central narrative elements: characterisation, plot, setting and performance style.

REPRODUCIBLE – PART TWO: SAMPLE PROJECTS YEAR 7 – 4. READING REIMAGINED

A lesson should be given reminding students of the correct way to structure a play script, as students will be expected to submit a polished version of their script for assessment.

REHEARSING THE PLAY

As students move into the rehearsal stage of this project, they should be encouraged to adopt roles such as actors, director, costume designer, technical director and set designer. When students begin blocking out their play, they will need to be supported by the teacher. Encourage the actors to annotate their copies of the script to identify appropriate places for:

- pauses
- emphasis
- volume
- gestures
- body language
- facial expressions.

To enhance their performance, students may wish to incorporate costumes, music or sound effects, make-up and props. They will need to make sure that these choices are appropriate to the mood and content of their play.

FORMATIVE ASSESSMENT 2

Below are some strategies you might like to use to check students' understanding and skills at this stage of the project.

- A checklist for a performance of a play script. A great activity is to have students develop the criteria for their own product. In this instance, they will be writing a play script AND performing the play. They will need separate checklists and criteria for each. Students should have a good knowledge of what makes a great script and performance, as they have engaged with a range of performance texts in the Discover stage of learning. Have students brainstorm 5–10 elements that a great script and a great performance must have. Use these to create a checklist for success. A blank checklist has been included for you in "Part 3: Additional Resources".

- Thirty-second check-ins. This formative assessment strategy is useful when students are working in their teams to compose their plays. Select a time during the lesson and stop students working. Ask for silence. Choose one student from each team to stand up in front of the class and share what their team is working on in just 30 seconds. Encourage them to share what they have achieved, what they have learned and what they still need to do in order to successfully complete their play.

- Use the Creative Thinking rubric for peer and self-assessment when students are at the play-building stage. The rubric can be found in the back of this book.

SHARE

Students will need to spend a number of lessons planning and rehearsing the performance of their plays. At this final stage, they may benefit from filming and watching back their performances, as this will help them identify elements that need to be strengthened.

This stage of a project, right before the final performance for the Foundation students, can be very stressful for students and you as their teacher. To alleviate some of this stress, ensure that all students understand their specific roles and responsibilities. It is a good idea to have a chart outlining these on your project wall. For example, make-up artists must ensure all make-up is prepared and ready for each actor. They are responsible for the make-up being at the venue for the performance.

Encourage students to get involved with organising the final performance event. They should give the event a catchy name — as silly as it seems, this will make it more valuable for your students. Give them some time to create flyers or invitations as well as posters or decorations for the venue. Instruct students to bring a plate of food as refreshments for the guests. You will also need to double-check that the guest expert and other invited guests are still able to attend the event (where appropriate).

FORMATIVE ASSESSMENT 3

Below are some strategies you might like to use to check students' understanding and skills at this stage of the project.

- It is important that students get feedback on their performance at least once before the final event. You might like to use a peer-assessment strategy like "star, star, wish" (students identify two things they thought were effective, and one element of the performance they wish was changed or added).
- After the performances, have each student write on a slip of paper which team performance they enjoyed the most, giving two reasons why they selected that team. Encourage them to support their selection with reasons from the criteria used for a performance at the create stage of the project.

YEAR 8

1. BODACIOUS BALLADEERS

PROJECT AT A GLANCE:

 **DRIVING QUESTION:** How can we, as balladeers, tell the tales of our town?

 DISCOVER: Students will read and listen to a range of contemporary and traditional ballads, as well as research stories from their local area.

 CREATE: Students will work in a team to write and record a ballad about their home town.

 SHARE: Students will plan and set up an exhibition of their ballads in the local public library. They will also plan and run an evening event opening the exhibition.

TAKE IT FURTHER: Ballads can be uploaded to the school or local council YouTube channel, or played on the local radio station.

 ASSESSMENT: Students will be assessed on their written and recorded ballads.

 21ST-CENTURY SKILLS: intercultural understanding, ethical understanding, creative thinking, research skills, collaboration and communication.

LITERACY: *grammar* – clauses, conjunctions, pronouns; *reading* – visualising, making predictions, summarising; *punctuation* – ellipses, commas, semicolons, dashes

TYPE OF TEXT: imaginative (ballad) and informative (report – optional)

LANGUAGE FEATURES OF TEXTS: allusion, evocative vocabulary, metaphor, enjambment, mood, tone and poetic devices; narrative elements – plot, characterisation, setting, theme, style

POSSIBLE TEXTS: *The Man from Snowy River* by Banjo Paterson (1890), *The Rime of the Ancient Mariner* by Samuel Taylor Coleridge (1798), *The Walrus and the Carpenter* and *The Jabberwocky* by Lewis Carroll (1871) and *Annabel Lee* by Edgar Allan Poe (1849).

A great source for information on ballads: https://www.britannica.com/art/ballad.

How can we, as balladeers, tell the tales of our town?

Discover:

- The history, language features and structure of the ballad form
- The works of talented balladeers from the past and the present
- Intriguing narratives from the history of your home town

Assessment: _____

Create:

- A ballad capturing one of the home-town stories you discovered
- A digital recording of your team's ballad, including music and/or sound effects

Assessment: _____

Share:

- Your ballad with your community at an exhibition at your local public library

Assessment: _____

REPRODUCIBLE — PART TWO: SAMPLE PROJECTS YEAR 8 — 1. BODACIOUS BALLADEERS

BEFORE YOU BEGIN

CONTACT EXPERTS/ROCK STARS

The strength of this project rests on the quality of the experts that you involve. Selecting an expert in advance is essential. Poetry is a difficult form for most students, however, this project is designed to make connections between a traditional poetic form, the ballad and your students' home town. Try your best to involve experts from the local historical society or the local council – they will help bring the history of your home town to life. You might also like to invite a spoken word poet (such as Omar Musa) to run a workshop with your students to help them produce a better-quality narrative poem in both the written and the oral forms. Another option for an expert could be an academic specialising in poetry from a university.

MODIFY PROJECT OUTLINE

A project outline has been given as a suggestion. You may like to use this outline as it is, but it is likely that you will need to modify it to match the needs of your specific students and context. Remember that PBL is all about engaging students through making content significant for their needs and interests – perhaps you will have a different driving question that better reflects the needs of your students. You will also need to modify the project outline to indicate due dates for formative and summative assessment.

ORGANISE PROJECT PACKETS

This is an important organisation strategy that we use a lot in PBL. For this project, students will be working in small teams. A project packet is a small folder or document wallet given to each team, containing all the essential materials for students to be successful with the project. These remain in the classroom and are accessed by students each lesson. Alternatively, you can use a digital project packet using a program like Google Drive.

PLAN PROJECT TEAMS

Planning teams is inherently difficult, as you must consider the personality as well as the skill level of each student in your class. For this project, it is best to select a mixed team, taking into consideration the following skills: critical thinking, creativity, ICT skills and public speaking. Try to balance the teams to ensure that you have even numbers of outgoing and reserved students.

CREATE SPACE FOR A PROJECT WALL

This project wall will need to be updated regularly so students can see their understanding of the play grow. Start your project wall with the title of the project: "Bodacious Balladeers". In equally large writing, put up your project's driving question – students need to see this as it will drive them through the project and inspire them to think critically. You will also need an A3 colour printout of the project outline. You may like to laminate the outline; we often do. Leave space on the wall for a project calendar (or put up a blank one and have a student fill it in as you negotiate due dates etc.), the Need to Know list of questions and a good amount of space for key terms. Remember that these spaces need to be blank at the beginning of the project, as students will add this information during the Discover stage of learning. Use as much colour as you can. It is important that students are attracted to the wall, as it is a visible record of their learning. You might even like to nominate a student to be responsible for adding new information to the "key terms" or Need to Know spaces.

LAUNCH YOUR PROJECT

HOOK LESSON

There are so many possibilities for how to hook your students' interest in this project. The first thing to consider is what the main conceptual focus of the project is; in this instance, it could be either the narrative structure or the town history. Another approach may focus on poetry as the most important element of the project. Below are two ways to approach the hook lesson for this project.

- Have students watch a range of music videos of songs that have an obvious narrative to them. Some that you might show are "Where the Wild Roses Grow" by Nick Cave and Kylie Minogue, "Bohemian Rhapsody" by Queen, "Cat's in the Cradle" by Harry Chapin and "Hurricane" by Bob Dylan. As students watch they can read the lyrics to the songs as well (all available online). Ask students to brainstorm as many single words as they can to describe the songs and write these words on the board. Ask students to make connections between the songs — drawing out the idea that they all have a strong narrative, including a central character and a developed plot.

- Another option might be to have students listen to and watch the clips for a range of love ballads. Some that you might show include "Unchained Melody" by Ronson and Jerome, "(Everything I Do) I Do it for You" by Bryan Adams, "I Will Always Love You" by Whitney Houston and "My Heart Will Go On" by Celine Dion. Put students in small teams and give each team the term "ballad". Get them to complete one of the following activities:
    - five-minute brain dump (everything they know about ballads)
    - five-minute internet research on ballads
    - five-minute star-bursting: the who/what/when/why/where of ballads.

POSE DRIVING QUESTION

The lesson after the hook lesson is very, very important. This is the lesson where students are given access to the project's driving question for the first time. This project's driving question is: *How can we, as balladeers, tell the tales of our town?* Of course, if you'd like to use another driving question, you certainly can.

Once you pose this question to the students (we often put it up on the whiteboard or the interactive whiteboard), get them to immediately write down their own unmediated personal response to it. This will become their hypothesis, which will be tested and reshaped as they work through the Discover learning stage.

HAND OUT PROJECT OUTLINE

We recommend that the project outline is printed off in colour or printed onto coloured paper. This sets it apart from other pieces of paper that students will receive or use during the project. The project outline is a very important document as it acts as a flyer for learning. As soon as you hand the project outline out, have students sit quietly and read through it, using a pen or highlighter to identify any information that they feel they do not understand or that they have questions about. This is an essential step, as this information becomes part of what the class identifies as what they need to know. It is a good idea to encourage students to keep this project outline in their team's project packet or their own personal portfolio. We have had great success with students keeping a personal plastic sleeve folder as their "learning portfolio". They will use this for the entire year or for all projects.

ESTABLISH NEED TO KNOW

This is such an integral part of PBL. PBL is about inquiry that is led by the students. One of the best ways to begin inquiry is to ask questions. Once students have considered the driving question and have read through the project outline, they will no doubt begin to ask a lot of questions. This is a good thing. Your job is to not answer the questions, but rather to encourage students to record and develop their questions further. Before you do this, take some time to get your students to focus on what they already DO know about the project, as well as what content knowledge and skills they can bring to it. This step is essential, as it gives you an initial understanding of where each student is at in terms of their prior knowledge – it doesn't make sense teaching content and skills they already have, does it? To support this process, we use a KWL table. Have students try to write down five things they KNOW about the project already – this will include things like knowing what they have to do (write a ballad and record it), when things are due and for whom they are creating their products. This information is on the project outline, but it's good to get them to transfer it to the "What I Know" column of the KWL table so you can see that they understand the task. The next step is to get them to write down any content knowledge or skills they already have that will help them succeed with the project – these might include things like being skilled at working with audio software and having an understanding of poetic devices. Make sure you go around and see what each student has written as this will help you know where and how to distribute your time during the project.

Now it's time to start recording those questions. You may like to do this as a class group – having students call out their questions and allocating one student the role of scribe. These questions can then be recorded onto the project wall, becoming a guide for students' learning through the project. If you think students need to develop their questioning strategies, you could try using the star-bursting technique. Have students draw a six-pointed star in the middle of a sheet of paper. On each point write: *where, what, how, when, why* and *which*. Encourage students to think of as many questions about the project (and its related content) beginning with each word, and record them on their paper. You will be surprised by the richness and diversity of the questions asked by students.

CREATE A PROJECT CALENDAR

A project calendar is designed to keep students forward-focused. PBL is a student-directed methodology where students are required to take responsibility for their own learning. As such, a project calendar can help students keep themselves organised and ensure that they are working towards clearly established deadlines. These deadlines should be negotiated with the teacher as a whole class; however, there will be times when individual teams will have different deadlines to ensure that learning is differentiated effectively. We recommend that a project calendar includes clearly identified dates for formative assessment, that is, assessment for learning through strategies like plans, drafts, mini-presentations, quizzes and meetings with team leaders. This project has students completing two products – a ballad and a recording of it. The project calendar must reflect opportunities for teams to receive feedback on these products at the process stage. Students will also negotiate with the teacher opportunities for direct instruction – this is where the teacher runs a traditional, teacher-centred lesson.

DISCOVER

The first thing to do with this project is to check students' prior knowledge about poetry. There are two possibilities for this:

1. In teams, students are to create a "picture of poetry" (words and images; colourful) that is annotated with everything they know about poetry. These are stuck up on the classroom walls for the class to see.
2. A quiz of poetic terms. Students can keep taking the test until they get 100% — mastery learning. This is a strategy using in PBL and encourages students to learn from their mistakes and to keep trying. Kahoot is great for mastery learning, and it's fun.

A significant amount of the Discover cycle of learning for this project will be teacher-driven. Before the poetry analysis, you might want to get students to work individually or in small teams to research the history of the ballad. Once they have a sufficient knowledge of the form, it is time to focus on the poetry analysis as a model for your students' own compositions. You may want to use the strategy outlined below, or you may have your own preferred method for modelling how to critically engage with poetry.

Select a poem to use as a model for the class. Tell the class that you are modelling the process of critical analysis. Ask them, "Why do you need to know this?" They should be able to say, "Because we have to write and record our own ballad."

Read the poem to the class. Pose the following questions: What is the poem about? Why was the poem written? Demonstrate how you use the "what I know" and "what I wonder" thinking strategy as you go through the poem — write these on the board.

Use a KWL table to support this and to encourage critical thinking. Model this by writing two or three things that you feel confident the students could identify as things they "know" about the poem from first reading. For example, they might know it is written in first-person, or where the narrative is set. Now write two or three "what I wonder" questions in the W column, e.g. "I wonder why the poet uses so many similes?" or "I wonder why the poem is structured in this way?" Give students an opportunity to try and answer your "what I wonder" questions. Together, come to a consensus on why the poem was written and what the poet is saying. A table has been included as a resource with this unit that you may wish to use with your students for their poetry analysis.

Now identify some poetic devices the poet uses to convey this meaning. Tell students that this is an important stage of critical thinking when analysing a poem. Just select about four or five poetic devices — enough to write two great paragraphs. On the board, use the information you have gathered through the class discussion to write two analytical paragraphs about the poem. This isn't meant to be a detailed analysis of a poem — just a quick lesson on how to do it. This can be quite an intimidating task to perform in front of the class, so you might want to prepare your analysis before the lesson so you feel more confident. These paragraphs will act as a model for what students need to produce themselves if you set an analytical essay or series of paragraphs for the Discover stage assessment.

Repeat the above process with at least one other ballad.

Lead a class discussion about what makes a good ballad, based on their study of published ballads. Co-construct a rubric for ballad writing with levels ranging from "great" to "awful". The "great" criteria become the checklist for student ballads. You should also take some this time to focus on the necessary features of a narrative – plot, setting, characterisation, theme and style.

The last aspect of the Discover stage of this project is to have students do some research into the history of their home town – your school's community. You may wish to take students on an excursion to the local public library to look at the archives and talk to the librarian about the town's history (with a special focus on interesting characters or stories), or you could invite someone from the local historical society to speak with your students. A final option might be to have students interview people from their community to find inspiration for their poems.

FORMATIVE ASSESSMENT 1

This project calls for some serious formative assessment strategies. We like to use end of lesson reflections using the "medals and missions" strategy – this sees students identifying one thing during that lesson that they mastered and one thing that they still need to master relating to the project. This is a simple but effective way of having students reflect on their learning.

Other formative assessment ideas:

- Have students write an individual or collaborative essay on the ballad form, including analysis of at least two ballads studied in class.
- Create a quiz based on the main features of ballads – make this a Kahoot to add extra competition and fun for students.
- Have students write a report or deliver a presentation on the history of the ballad form.

Name the Poetic Technique

You have been given examples of poetic techniques. Write the poetic device that has been used next to the example.

You eat like a pig. _____

You are a pig. _____

Ladies like lovely lipstick. _____

The fingers of the vine grabbed at her hair. _____

As blind as a bat. _____

The rain in Spain stays mainly on the plain. _____

The bug crunched under his thumping boot. _____

"All the world's a stage and all the men and women merely players."

_____

"Life is like a box of chocolates. You never know what you're gonna get."

_____

The siren wailed. _____

Her eyes shone like diamonds. _____

He wolfed down his dinner. _____

The river was choking on the rubbish. _____

Slowly, silently and stealthily he crept. _____

You missed the target by a mile. _____

He was a wise fool. _____

As the battle reached its climax, the terrifying storm erupted in the sky.

_____

Poetry Analysis Table

What is the theme of this ballad?				
What poetic devices are being used to say this in the poem?				
What is an example of this device being used?				
What does this device make you think, feel or imagine relating to the poem's theme?				
Why is this theme important to people in the world? Restate the main idea of the paragraph.				

CREATE 🎵

It is now time for the students to decide what local story they would like to tell in their ballad. Remind them that this part of the project is paramount to creating an effective poem, as they want to ensure their story has strong characterisation, plot and themes to engage their listeners. Once a story has been decided upon, students should begin brainstorming the structure of their ballad in teams. Encourage students to use the ballad checklist based on the "great" criteria that the class devised in earlier lessons. A blank checklist is in "Part Three: Additional Resources". Students should receive feedback and feed-forward from at least one other team on their final narrative idea before beginning to write their first draft. It is a good idea for the teacher to model how to use the checklist, how to annotate a draft and how to give "medals and missions" feedback/feed-forward. There is information on this process in "A Word About PBL and Assessment" on page 19. Students submit their final ballads to you for teacher feedback. A sample student-created ballad can be found on page 97.

Allow students to spend a few minutes looking at the project calendar and seeing what goals have been met and what needs to be changed. They will likely identify that it is time to begin work on the digital recording of their ballad. This process of reflection on learning helps students to celebrate their hard work. Learning is hard!

In teams, students negotiate roles and responsibilities for the digital recording. Teams will need to decide who will read the poem (it can be more than one student) as well as what music and/or sound effects they should include to add to the mood of their poem. Students will then need to conduct some hands-on learning as they work out the best software and hardware to use for recording their poems. You should work with individual teams to guide them through the process. Don't worry if you don't know how to create a digital recording, just relax and learn with your students. An example can be seen on page 98.

Students will also need to be given some time to learn how to create QR codes that their audience can scan in order to hear the poem recordings. This is a very easy process and there are a lot of helpful tutorials online, so be patient and enjoy learning this new skill with your students.

FORMATIVE ASSESSMENT 2

Below are some strategies you might like to use to check students' understanding and skills at this stage of the project. These are typically tasks completed in the last 5–10 minutes of a lesson.

- Give each student two different coloured pieces of paper about the size of a postcard. On one piece, students write something they feel they can confidently teach their peers relating to the product (ballad) or the driving question. On the other piece, students write something they would like help with relating to the product (ballad) or the driving question. These are put into separate boxes for the next lesson.
- Thirty-second share – each student stands up and shares one thing they have discovered about poetry/a poet/the driving question. Encourage students to share original ideas and avoid repeating what other students have already shared. Celebrate their learning with some type of reward.
- On a piece of paper, students are to identify who they think is working the most and the least in their team.
- Students can give peer feedback based on their ballad checklist – encourage them to use the language of the criteria for their feedback.

The Ballad of Freshwater Beach

By Katelin, Barr, Reece and Nell

Freshwater's name came to be,
when a creek was discovered leading into the sea.

By Freshwater will always remember that day
when surfing was born in the fresh water bay.

One early morning in the year nineteen fifteen,
one Duke Kahanamoku rode the first wave
Australia had seen.

It was late summer when he paddled through the surf,
And out he sat and watched his luscious turf.

When the time came upon him he paddled on a wave,
And there he stood tall and proud like in a quiet cave.

When he walked up to the beach, he scoured the crowd,
For one to join him on the water and shout out loud.

When the first Australian rode on the board
The whole of the town cheered in applause.

From the day on the village by the sand
was well known as the place where surfing began.

Want to hear a reading of this poem by the poets themselves?

Download a QR reader to your smart phone (there are many free versions such as Red Laser, Barcode Scanner and QR Scanner) and scan the QR code below.

The Ballad of Freshwater Beach
By Katelin, Barr, Reece and Nell

> QR or Quick response Codes are type of two-dimensional barcode that can be read using smartphones and dedicated QR reading devices that link directly to text emails, websites and more!

SHARE

PRESENTATION OF DIGITAL RECORDINGS

Rehearsing is so important at this stage. No-one wants to listen to a boring or badly recorded ballad. Students should work as a team to rehearse and record their ballad. Work with individual teams to guide them through the process. The quality of sound is important, so make sure you allow enough time for students to experiment with the audio recording software they have chosen to use. This will ensure a better-quality product. If you don't have laptops or tablets, this will require accessing a computer room, so make sure you book this well in advance.

If you have chosen to hold an evening "opening" of the ballad exhibition in the library, devote some time to preparing students for the event. Students should take time to prepare for the presentation of recorded ballads to invited guests. Ensure each team rehearses a very brief introductory speech and checks that their recording is ready to be heard. Organise a student to open the event with a brief overview of the project and an introduction of your guests. Your guests might like to speak briefly about their experiences with poetry or local history.

FORMATIVE ASSESSMENT

Below are some strategies you might like to use to check students' understanding and skills at this stage of the project.

- Have students complete the "L" column of the KWL table they were working on at the beginning of the project.
- Use class-created criteria for presentation and peer assessment of ballads.

POST-PROJECT REFLECTION/EVALUATION

After the setting up of the ballad exhibition and the presentation of the ballads, have a class "celebration of project success" lesson with lollies or chips and music. Use the beginning of that lesson to have students evaluate the project and their learning by completing the "Bodacious Balladeers" reflection questions below.

BODACIOUS BALLADEERS REFLECTION

1. One of the learning goals of this project was to be able to write a bodacious ballad. How well did you achieve this goal?
2. During this project, you engaged with some complex poetry. Which poem did you find the most challenging? Why?
3. What ICT skills did you develop as a result of creating a digital recording of your ballad?
4. What is something that was hard for you at the start of the project, but is easy now?
5. This project aimed to develop your appreciation for how poetry can capture stories. How has your appreciation of poetry developed?
6. What in our class has made the biggest impact on your learning during this project? Why?
7. What is something the teacher could have done to make this project better?
8. If you could turn back time and do this project again, what would you do differently?

YEAR 8
2. AWESOME AUTEURS

PROJECT AT A GLANCE:

 **DRIVING QUESTION:** How can we pay homage to our favourite auteurs through a three-minute film?

 DISCOVER: Students will research the biography and context of a specific auteur, as well as watching and analysing a range of films by the auteur.

 CREATE: Students will individually write a feature article about the life and work of the auteur, and in teams they will script, film and edit a three-minute short film.

 SHARE: Students will publish their feature articles in a class collection and screen their short film at an evening for family, friends and the general public.

TAKE IT FURTHER: Organise for the film screenings to take place at a local cinema; send links to the videos online to the auteur they studied; invite other local secondary schools to participate in the film festival.

 ASSESSMENT: Feature article (individual) and short film (team).

 21ST-CENTURY SKILLS: critical thinking, creative thinking, ICT use and collaboration

LITERACY: *grammar* – noun types and noun clauses, passive voice, sentence types; *reading* – summarising, making connections, predicting; *punctuation* – colons, semicolons, parentheses

TYPE OF TEXT: informative (feature article) and imaginative (short film)

LANGUAGE FEATURES OF TEXTS: film – shot types (long, mid, close-up, extreme close-up, establishing shot), angle types (high, low, overhead, eye level, birds-eye, Dutch tilt), camera movement (pan, tilt, tracking, dolly), editing (wipe, fade, cut, jump cut), sound (diegetic, non-diegetic), lighting (high key, low key, backlighting), symbolism, costuming and motif

POSSIBLE AUTEURS: Tim Burton, Alfred Hitchcock, Steven Spielberg, Hayao Miyazaki, Spike Jonze, Sophia Coppola, Nora Ephron, Jodie Foster.

HOW CAN WE PAY HOMAGE TO OUR FAVOURITE AUTEURS THROUGH A THREE-MINUTE FILM?

DISCOVER:
- The biography and context of a chosen auteur
- The distinctive features of the auteur
- At least two of the auteur's films

CREATE:
- A feature article discussing what makes the auteur's work distinctive
- A three-minute short film that pays homage to the auteur

SHARE:
- Your feature article in a collection called "Awesome Auteurs"
- Your short film with a public audience at the Awesome Auteurs Film Fest

ASSESSSMENT

ASSESSMENT

ASSESSMENT

BEFORE YOU BEGIN

CONTACT EXPERTS/ROCK STARS

This project requires your students to create a short film for inclusion in a film festival. You may choose to give your students a choice about who they would prefer to be in the audience, or you might find it more effective to specify the audience for them. If you choose to specify the audience and include guests from outside the school, you will likely need to organise invitations to go out quite early in the project, if not before the project begins. Possible guests include local filmmakers, students studying film at university, academics who specialise in film or the film reviewer from the local newspaper.

This project also requires students to write a feature article about the life and work of an auteur. In order to make this part of the project engaging, you might wish to invite in an expert to speak about writing for magazines or newspapers, or writing critical responses to film. Academics or journalists from the local newspaper would be an excellent choice for this role.

MODIFY PROJECT OUTLINE

Look at the sample project outline given. Remember that PBL is all about engaging students through making content significant for their needs and interests. You will also need to modify the project outline to indicate due dates for formative and summative assessment.

ORGANISE PROJECT PACKETS

This is an important organisation strategy that we use a lot in PBL. For this project, students will be working in small teams. A project packet is a small folder or document wallet given to each team that contains all the essential materials for students to be successful with the project. These packets remain in the classroom and are accessed by students each lesson. Of course, there are so many technology options available that your project packets do not need to be paper-based. The benefits of having digital project packets and ePortfolios mean that you and the students can add to and access them from home. Some of the online tools that would be great for this application include: Google Drive, Blackboard, Edmodo, Glogster, Weebly, Evernote and Canvas.

PLAN PROJECT TEAMS

Planning teams is inherently difficult, as you must consider the personality as well as the skill level of each student in your class. For this project, it is best to select a mixed team, taking into consideration the following skills: creative writing, leadership skills, performance skills and technological skills, such as using the video camera and editing the film. Try to balance the teams to ensure that you have even numbers of outgoing and reserved students. The short films may require students to act in front of their peers, and this may be daunting for many students. Add to that knowing that this film will be screened for a public audience, and students are going to need to feel supported and comfortable. As such, try to ensure each student has at least one person they trust and are on friendly terms with in their team.

CREATE SPACE FOR A PROJECT WALL

This project wall will need to be updated regularly so students can see their understanding of the auteur's style grow. Start your project wall with the title of the project: "Awesome Auteurs". The term *auteur* is a contested one, so perhaps you can have a discussion focused on why it is controversial. In equally large writing, put up your project's driving question – students need to see this as it will drive them through the project and inspire them to think critically. You will also need an A3 colour printout of the project outline. Leave space for a project calendar (or put up a blank one and have a student fill it in as you negotiate due dates, etc.), the Need to Know list of questions and a good amount of space for key terms. Since this is a project exploring auteur theory and film it won't take long to identify new words and terms that students previously did not know. Remember that these spaces need to be blank at the beginning of the project, as this information will be added by students during the Discover stage of learning. Use as much colour as you can – it is important that students are attracted to the wall as it is a visible record of their learning. You might even like to nominate a student to be responsible for adding new information to the "key terms" or Need to Know spaces. If you don't happen to have your own classroom and therefore can't add information to a physical wall, how about creating a digital project wall? Online tools like Glogster, Weebly and Canvas are great for this purpose.

LAUNCH YOUR PROJECT

HOOK LESSON

There are so many possibilities for how to hook your students' interest in this project. The best idea is to base it on the style of the selected auteur. Below are some ideas for hook lessons if you choose Burton as the focus auteur.

- Draw weird creatures from different starting images (like Mr. Squiggle used to do!).
- Write silly poems like "Stick Boy and Match Girl".
- Match the title of a Tim Burton film to its main character.

POSE DRIVING QUESTION

The lesson after the hook lesson is very important. This is the lesson where students are given access to the project's driving question for the first time. This project's driving question is: *How can we pay homage to our favourite auteurs through a three-minute film?*

Of course, it's also a great activity to get students to design the project's driving question with you. This can be done through a class discussion. We have done this a number of times with our classes and it is always surprising what students come up with. When they have ownership over part of the project design, they feel ownership of their learning.

Once you pose this question to the students (we often put it up on the whiteboard or the interactive whiteboard), get each individual to immediately write down their own unmediated personal response to it. This will become their hypothesis, which will be tested and reshaped as they work through the Discover learning stage.

HAND OUT PROJECT OUTLINE

We recommend that the project outline is printed off in colour or printed onto coloured paper. This sets it apart from other pieces of paper that they will receive or use during the project. The project outline is a very important document as it acts as a flyer for learning. As soon as you hand the project outline out, have students sit quietly and read through it, using a pen or highlighter to identify any information that they feel they do not understand or about which they have questions. This is an essential step, as this information becomes part of what the class identifies as what they need to know. It is a good idea to encourage students to keep this project outline in their team's project packet or their own personal portfolio. We have had great success with students keeping a personal plastic sleeve folder as their "learning portfolio". If you have access to devices like PCs, tablets or laptops, you might consider having students create digital portfolios using programs such as Google Drive or OneDrive. Students will use their portfolio for the entire year of projects.

ESTABLISH NEED TO KNOW

The Need to Know is such an integral part of PBL. PBL is about inquiry that is led by the students. One of the best ways to begin inquiry is to ask questions. Once students have considered the driving question and have read through the project outline, they will no doubt begin to ask a lot of questions. This is a good thing. Your job is to not answer the questions, but rather to encourage students to record and develop their questions further. You may like to do this as a class group — having students call out their questions and allocating one student the role of scribe. These questions can then be recorded onto the project wall, becoming a guide for students' learning through the project. If you think students need to develop their questioning strategies, you could try using the star-bursting technique. Have students draw a six-pointed star in the middle of a sheet of paper. On each point write: *where, what, how, when, why* and *who*. Encourage students to think of as many questions as possible about the project (and its related content) beginning with each word, and record them on their paper. You will be surprised by the richness and diversity of the questions students ask. This lesson also provides an opportunity for students to begin thinking about the audience for their presentation and product. For example: *Who will it be? What are their interests? How do we cater for these interests?* Note that these questions will stem from the original driving question, which must be strong and have the potential to generate further questions and set the stage for students' inquiry. Look at the example from the Game 2 Learn project on page 27.

SET UP TEAMS

This is a fairly quick step in PBL, but it can be very painful for students. Most students will initially resent being "forced" to work with peers with whom they don't usually associate. This is normal. Our experience is that after the first few projects, students become much more accustomed to working with a range of peers, and even begin to acknowledge the strengths of others they may not usually work with. As a teacher, you need to think about what the benefits will be to having students working in teams for a specific project. The obvious reason is that we want to develop teamwork skills such as collaboration, communication and collective decision-making, however, other valid reasons include appreciating diversity in learning styles and deepening understanding by considering a range of perspectives on an issue. When student teams are first established, it is a good idea to encourage them to choose a team name — this gives them a collective identity. Try to remember the team names and refer to each team by their name at some point during each lesson. We find it handy to run a team-building activity, such as having students devise a team contract where they commit to certain expected behaviours like being on time to class, not interrupting when someone else is talking or putting in their personal best for each lesson. You might like to provide your students with a scaffold for this, and we've provided you with an example in the "Part Three: Additional Resources" section of this book. Routine is very important to PBL, so encourage students to select someone in the team to be responsible for collecting the team's project packet each lesson and one member to be the team spokesperson for when they need to share ideas with the teacher or the class.

CREATE A PROJECT CALENDAR

A project calendar is designed to keep students forward-focused. PBL is a student-directed methodology, where students are required to take responsibility for their own learning. As such, a project calendar can help students keep themselves organised and ensure that they are working towards clearly established deadlines. These deadlines should be negotiated with the teacher as a whole class, however, there will be times when individual teams will have different deadlines to ensure that learning is differentiated effectively. We recommend that a project calendar includes clearly identified dates for formative assessment, that is, assessment for learning through strategies like plans, drafts, mini presentations, quizzes and meetings with team leaders. This project has students completing two products — a feature article and a short film. The project calendar must reflect opportunities for teams to receive feedback on these products at the process stage. Students will also negotiate with the teacher opportunities for direct instruction — this is where the teacher runs a traditional, teacher-centred lesson — and time to receive and apply feedback. For this project, students are required to engage with the works of an auteur, and therefore a number of lessons will need to be dedicated to whole-class instruction while the films are viewed and analysed.

DISCOVER

GETTING TO KNOW THE AUTEUR AND THE FILMS

This project has an extended inquiry phase because students must engage with a number of films or artistic works. Of course, how you decide to get your students to engage with the texts is up to you. It is also highly dependent on your students. Some teachers will want their students to engage with the biography and style of the auteur as a whole class by engaging with resources found mostly by the teacher. Other teachers will want their students to do independent research to discover the life and style of the auteur. Furthermore, some teachers will have the class watch two or three entire films, while others may only watch excerpts of the films. This decision will depend on the time available, as well as the selected auteur, as some films may not be suitable for students to watch in their entirety within the school context. Through a process of inquiry, whether that is guided or independent, students are required to discover the distinctive stylistic features of the selected auteur, as well as the biographical and contextual information that influenced the development of this distinctive style. See over the page for a worksheet to support students' viewing and analysis of the set films. There is also a "Research and Respond" handout for a project on Tim Burton which can be modified for your students if you select a different auteur. There are some excellent print resources to support a study of Tim Burton as auteur, these include: *Burton on Burton* (1995), *Tim Burton: The Exhibition* by Ron Magliozzi and Jenny He (2010), *The Nightmare Before Christmas*, by Tim Burton (1993), *The Melancholy Death of Oyster Boy & Other Stories* (1997). A great animated series created by Burton, *Stainboy* (2000), can be found online.

GETTING TO KNOW THE STRUCTURE AND LANGUAGE OF A FEATURE ARTICLE

At some point your students will have identified that they need to know how to write a feature article. This provides them with an opportunity to book in the teacher to deliver a whole-class lesson of some description. This could be a lively class discussion, a series of collaborative activities or an opportunity for the teacher to provide students with written information about personal essays. When supporting students with their discovery of a new type of text, it is important to spend time looking at the language features specific to this type of text, as well as the spelling, punctuation and grammar with which students will likely need support. While it is highly likely that you will identify common weaknesses in these basics when you're reading initial drafts, it is still a good idea to front-load by addressing likely errors before they occur.

RESPONDING TO A PRESCRIBED TEXT

Base your answers to the questions below on the text you have studied in class. Remember to pay attention to the types of VERBS used in each question.

1. Identify the main characters and settings in the text.

   _____
   _____

2. Describe the plot of your text.

   _____
   _____

3. Explain the main theme of your text.

   _____
   _____

4. Analyse how the composer has used the elements of narrative to communicate their main theme

   _____
   _____

REPRODUCIBLE – PART TWO: SAMPLE PROJECTS YEAR 8 – 2. AWESOME AUTEURS

RESEARCH AND RESPOND

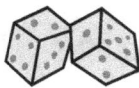 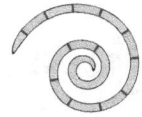

TASK ONE: Read through the biographical information about Tim Burton on his Wikipedia page. The page can be found by going to the main Wikipedia page and searching for "Tim Burton" (<https://en.wikipedia.org/wiki/Tim_Burton>). Remember, as you read you should identify the words you don't know and find out their meaning.

Answer the questions below

1. Where did Tim Burton grow up?
2. What is a "conceptual artist"?
3. Why do you think Burton was not successful in this job at Disney?
4. How did Burton get the job as director of *Pee-wee's Big Adventure*?
5. What was Burton's first blockbuster film?
6. Which famous actor starred in *Charlie and the Chocolate Factory*?
7. What inspired the film *Frankenweenie*?
8. Which of the films listed on the Wikipedia page have you seen?

TASK TWO: Now that you know about Tim Burton's biography and his personal artistic vision, it's time to look at some of his art. Read some of his poetry and look at some of his visual art — paintings, drawings and photographs. You can find examples of his visual art on his website: <http://timburton.com/>. As a class, discuss this question: *What makes the art of Tim Burton distinctive? Is his art so similar between his works that it lacks originality?*

TASK THREE: It's now the fun part of the project — watching movies! We all know how to watch films (it's pretty easy) but not everyone knows how to watch a film critically. Being a critical viewer means that you can appreciate *how* the director has used film techniques to shape our response to characters, situations and settings. A critical viewer can identify how the combination of creepy music, dark lighting and a slow tracking shot can make us feel a sense of suspense and maybe even fear in a specific scene. An even more critical viewer can evaluate the strengths and weaknesses of a film by judging what film techniques work to get the intended response and which ones fail completely. For example, if the audience laughs in a scene that is meant to be scary, the director has failed in his intention to create fear and suspense.

In class, you will watch four different films directed by Tim Burton. It is important that you watch these films with a critical eye and take note of how Burton uses film techniques to shape your response to settings, characters and events. You will notice that he often uses very similar techniques in his films!

REPRODUCIBLE – PART TWO: SAMPLE PROJECTS YEAR 8 – 2 . AWESOME AUTEURS

FORMATIVE ASSESSMENT 1

During the above inquiry, it is essential that you take frequent opportunities to check for understanding. There are many formative assessment strategies that can be used, however, some are more suited to this project than others. The following formative assessment strategies should be used during the inquiry stage of the project to help you assess for students' understanding.

- A multiple-choice quiz on the film's characters, plot and themes
- A team mini presentation focusing on one aspect of the auteur's distinctive style (characters, plot, symbolism, visual style, settings, themes)
- Exit slips asking students to summarise the scenes from the film watched in class that lesson
- A matching activity where students match a feature article language feature with its definition
- Give each team one or two of the Need to Know questions from the project wall and have them try to answer them, then sharing their answers with the class

If you discover that there is a gap in students' knowledge or understanding, then take the time to address this as well as you can. If it is a problem experienced by the class, address it as a whole class. If it is a problem experienced by a few students, bring them together in a small team and chat with them about ways to address the issue. This can be done while the rest of the class is working on an activity, either individually or in their project teams.

CREATE ♬

This part of the project should take approximately half of the time allocated for the completion of the project. Students will spend time planning and drafting their feature article. Once each student has written a draft, time should be given for peer feedback using a peer-feedback checklist. For best practice regarding the use of this checklist, read the information on assessment and PBL in this book on page 19. Once students have given and received peer feedback, they should spend some time refining their feature articles based on the suggestions of their peers, and their teacher if time permits. Final feature articles can be printed in a bound collection, posted online to share with a wider audience or published using an online book publisher like Blurb.

Now that students have a solid appreciation of the films, they will begin working in teams on their short film. Creating a short film is a time-consuming process, and will involve a lot of trial and error. In some lessons, it will appear as if students are achieving nothing – this is usually the scriptwriting and storyboarding stage – and others are a rush of action, especially when filming. On the following pages there is a brief handout that will support your students through the early planning stages of the filmmaking. Ensure students understand the stages of filmmaking: ideating, selection of the idea, scriptwriting, revising the script based on feedback, storyboarding, filming and editing. Formative assessment continues throughout this process, as you now have the opportunity to spend time with each team and help with their performance. You can find a checklist for a short film on page 53 as part of the #LoveOzYA project which can be modified for this project. Alternatively, co-constructing criteria with your class based on their viewing and analysis of the auteur's films gives students even greater ownership of the quality and judgement of their final product.

Finally, to help students stay on task, and ensure work is evenly distributed throughout the teams and completed on time, have students use the Project Management Log, found on page 54.

IT'S TIME TO MAKE A SHORT FILM THAT WILL IMPRESS TIM BURTON

Who is my film crew? _____

What role in filmmaking is each person most interested in? Put the names of the interested person beside each role — you can take turns and/or double up on roles. Every role needs to be allocated to a crew member.

Director
_____

Set/Costume Design
_____

Camera Operator
_____

Editor
_____

Sound/Music
_____

Lighting
_____

Acting
_____

Make-up Artist
_____

REPRODUCIBLE – PART TWO: SAMPLE PROJECTS YEAR 8 – 2 . AWESOME AUTEURS

1. The first thing to do is to decide as a team what parts of Tim Burton's personal style you will include in your film. Select your choices from the options below by circling or highlighting your choice.

GENRE

- Romance
- Horror
- Dark comedy
- Gothic

CAMERA WORK

- Free-floating camera to establish mood and setting
- Overhead and establishing shots for setting
- Tracking shots for action scenes
- High and low angles to show power/status of characters
- Close-ups and extreme close-ups to show character emotions
- Mid shots and long shots to establish character personalities

LIGHTING

- Low-key lighting to create heavy, dark shadows
- High-key lighting to create a bright, happy mood
- Backlighting to make a character look serious or threatening
- Contrast between black and white and colour to show the different worlds or characters

THEMES

- The power of the imagination
- The need to accept those who are different
- The valuing of individuality
- The impact of isolation on an individual
- The need to be loved
- The absurdity of "normal" society

CHARACTERS

- An outsider who is different but we like and feel sorry for
- A bad guy who we don't like (usually "normal")
- A good guy who helps the outsider (usually "normal")
- The lovers
- The "extras" who contribute to the mood or theme of the film

MUSIC

- Dramatic choir music to create a mysterious mood
- String music to create a romantic mood
- Fast-paced or increasing tempo music to create tension
- Silly music (like crazy jazz) to create humour
- Dramatic sound effects (like storms)

SYMBOLS

- Dead dog
- Chequered floors
- Contrast between dark world and colour world
- Skeletons
- Spirals
- Christmas/Halloween/winter
- Graveyards

 REPRODUCIBLE – PART TWO: SAMPLE PROJECTS YEAR 8 – 2. AWESOME AUTEURS

2. Now it is time to consider the style of your short film.
- Puppets
- Claymation
- Stop-motion animation
- Cartoon/animation
- Live-action (with actors)

_____
_____
_____
_____
_____
_____

3. Now it is time to start brainstorming your film.
- What will be the plot?
- Who will be the characters?
- Where will it be set?
- Use an A3 piece of paper to brainstorm as a group.

_____
_____
_____
_____
_____
_____
_____

SHARE

You and your students have finally made it to the end of the project. This part of the project will be both stressful and rewarding. Remember that your students are just as anxious at this stage as you are. It is essential that you give your students lots of encouragement and support, but don't fall into the trap of doing the work for them. It doesn't matter if their final product isn't perfect; it simply needs to be a reflection of their learning and effort as a team. At least one week before the Awesome Auteurs Film Fest, make sure that you have a good idea about who will be attending and that you have the ideal space for the film festival booked. Performance spaces don't need to be formal or fancy – if you can't book the local cinema, be creative by turning everyday spaces into a theatre, such as your classroom with the windows blacked out, or out on the school oval with a curtain or sheet as the screen.

SUMMATIVE ASSESSMENT

Remind students that they will be assessed on their film as a team or as individuals – whichever you choose – and that you will be using a checklist to give them feedback. It is important that students get a copy of the short film checklist (page 53) while they are preparing their film so that they understand the success criteria. Enjoy the show!

POST-PROJECT REFLECTION/EVALUATION

Reflection on learning is an integral part of PBL. The best type of reflection is highly defined and focused on the specific learning targets for the project. Ensure your reflection questions allow students to reflect on their development of these skills and capacities. This will allow them to draw a connection between what their goals were, what they did and how they grew as learners. There are so many ways that you can get your students to engage in reflection on their learning. You might get them to record a podcast describing their most and least favourite experiences during the project. You could get students to sit together in small groups and share three skills they've mastered and three new facts they've learned. Two students could interview each other and record their reflections for the teacher to read later. We get our students to blog a lot using the "think, puzzle, explore" method. For this project, get your students to reflect on their experience of this project by answering the questions below. You could have them put their answers in their portfolio to keep as a record of their learning, or they could use one of the other strategies mentioned above.

YEAR 8
3. LIFE STORIES

PROJECT AT A GLANCE:

 **DRIVING QUESTION:** Whose moment of change will I preserve in the amber of narrative?

 DISCOVER: Students will read a novel that explores the concept of change, learn the features of a short story and do independent research into a significant moment of change in the life of a loved one.

 CREATE: Students will write a short story based on their research into the life of a loved one.

 SHARE: Students' stories will be published in a collection titled *Moments of Change* and celebrate their success at a book launch with family and friends.

 ASSESSMENT: short story

 21ST-CENTURY SKILLS: ICT, digital citizenship, communication, collaboration, critical thinking, empathy, intercultural understanding

LITERACY: grammar – clause combinations, technicality and abstractions; spelling – nominalisations; punctuation – layout and font; reading – monitoring and making connections

TYPE OF TEXT: persuasive (advertising campaign) and imaginative (play)

LANGUAGE FEATURES OF TEXTS: characterisation, narrative structure, setting, genre, symbolism and motif, dialogue, figurative language

POSSIBLE AUTEURS: *Absolutely True Diary of a Part-time Indian* by Sherman Alexie (2007), *Wonder* by R.J. Palacio (2012), *Divergent* by Veronica Roth (2011), *The Protected* by Claire Zorn (2014), *Laurinda* by Alice Pung (2014), *The First Third* by Will Kostakis (2013), *The Freedom Ride* by Sue Lawson (2015), *Harry Potter and the Philosopher's Stone* by J.K. Rowling (1997), *Green Valentine* by Lili Wilkinson (2015)

Whose moment of change will I preserve in the amber of narrative?

Discover:
- The concept of change and the impact it has on individuals, society and humanity as a whole
- How the author of a novel uses narrative elements to capture transformative experiences
- The significant moments of change in the life of one of your loved ones

Assessment:

Create:
- A narrative based on an important moment of change in the life of a loved one

Assessment:

Share:
- Your completed narrative in a bound anthology titled *Moments of Change* and share it with family, friends and invited guests at a book launch

Assessment:

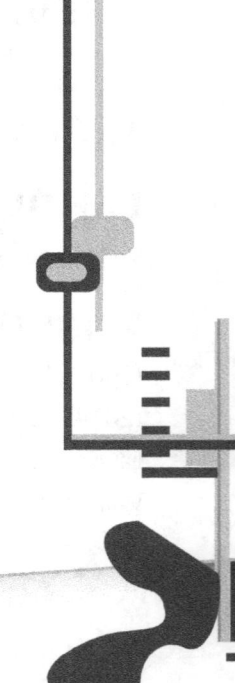

 REPRODUCIBLE – PART TWO: SAMPLE PROJECTS YEAR 8 – 3. LIFE STORIES

BEFORE YOU BEGIN

CONTACT EXPERTS

This project requires that you take a risk and connect with people from outside of your school. If not, the project won't work. Why not? Well, the narratives students write are actually based on the lived experiences of a chosen loved one, and they are also the audience for the final product. Asking young people to interview their loved ones might seem a bit stressful initially, but once they have spoken with them about the project, it will become a source of excitement and engagement for your students. You may also like to get an author to come and speak with your students about the writing process – this could happen in the Discover stage, or at the beginning of the Create stage. Many Australian authors can be contacted via social media, via their own blogs, or via their publisher or agent. Don't forget to invite the author back for the book launch at the end of the project!

PLAN THE HOOK LESSON

Writing short stories should be an engaging yet challenging experience for your students. To pique their interest in this project, you could use any of the following activities.

- A series of fun games like "Celebrity Heads", "Match the character to their fictional world" or "Match the author to the novel"
- Storytelling games, including writing "one sentence at a time" stories (Students write a sentence on a piece of paper, fold it over and pass it to another student to write a sentence. This continues until the end of the piece of paper. Stories end up being ridiculous but funny!); Rory's Story Cubes (You can buy these in toyshops and bookshops. Each dice has a little picture on it, students roll the dice and then they must tell a story based on the images that they roll. It's so much fun!); or have students select – at random – a character, setting and complication that they must use to tell a story through mime or tableaux
- Creating a gallery of baby or childhood images of the students or teachers, and have students guess who each one is

DISCOVER

Have students work individually and in pairs to complete the K and W columns of a KWL table about this project. Use the "W" questions as your focus Need to Know questions, and ensure they are put on your project wall for the students to use as a guide for their learning. An example list of Need to Know questions can be found in the resources for this stage of the project. Our students wrote these questions in the second lesson of the project, just after they were given the project outline. Seeing our students' ideas will hopefully help you to see how students should be supported to generate their own questions about the project.

Students will need to do some research into the significant moments of change in the life of their loved one and try to develop a sense of which one would be most suitable to explore in their short story. Be sure to remind students that they are writing a short story, not a memoir or biography, so they can elaborate upon the change experienced by their loved one – as long as they have sought permission to embellish or change aspects. You may wish to support students' research by giving them a scaffold for their findings. Students may find the resource on the following pages helpful, as it will ensure they have enough specific detail to create a realistic portrait of their loved one.

A main part of this inquiry stage of the project is the study of a novel that explores the concept of change. Your students should have identified this as an essential Need to Know when you first presented them with the project outline. Engaging with the novel's ideas, style, structure and language features will help students with the writing of their own short stories. You may wish to give the "Life Stories Matrix" resource to your students to help them record their ideas about the novel as they read it. Remember, you may choose to read the novel as a whole class, or you may want to set chapters for students to read independently at home.

FORMATIVE ASSESSMENT 1

Below are some strategies you might like to use to check students' understanding and skills at this stage of the project.

- A short quiz on the setting, characters, plot, stylistic features and themes of the novel
- Analytical paragraphs on the novel's exploration of change
- Students' submission of interview questions and answers
- Have students write a brief biography of their loved one
- The completed Life Story Worksheet
- Self-assessment using SOLO taxonomy (see "Part Three: Additional Resources" for more information)

LIFE STORIES – NEED TO KNOW QUESTIONS

This is an example list of possible Need to Know questions generated by students.

NOTE: These questions were produced by the students as a whole class. They identified whether the questions were focused on skills (S), content (C) or the project (P).

- What techniques are the most effective at conveying change? (S)
- What sort of changes can we expect to explore within the short story? (C)
- Who are some authors that would be willing to help us? (P)
- What sort of genres should be explored; should we all stick to one or branch out? (C)
- Who is our target audience? This will affect what is in our stories. (C)
- How can change be conveyed through a short story? (S)
- What literary techniques can be used to compose an entertaining, life-changing short story? (S)

- How can stories influence individuals to change an aspect of their life? (C)
- Should the short story be fiction or nonfiction? (P)
- How long will we have in class to write our story? (P)
- What exactly are we going to write about? (C)
- What is the best perspective to write in if we want the story to explore change? (S)
- What aspects of change do we include? (S and P)
- Do we need to write in a specific genre? (P)
- Whose life are we changing? (P)
- Will we get class time to write the narrative? (P)
- How do we incorporate change into a short story? (S)

- Why does change occur? (C)
- How many lessons do we have to plan our book? (P)
- How many lessons do we have to write our book? (P)
- When are our books due? (P)
- Is change the only requirement for what we need to write about? (C)
- How are we to publish this book? (P)
- Will the stories have any content in common, other than the element of change? (P)
- Who will be able to assist us with the editing and composition of the story? (S)
- What age group are we aiming this book to be for? (P)
- How can we express change through a story? (S)
- What genres or themes influence readers the most? (C)
- How can we effectively convey change in a short story? (S)
- How can changing someone's life affect others? (C)
- What length should they be? (P)
- Do picture books or comics count? (S)
- What are the marking criteria? (P)
- What genres are the most effective to inspire people? (C)
- Discuss whether the story should be lighthearted or dark and have "feels"? (P)
- Should the story's main character belong after change? (C)
- Why is it vital for a short story to change someone's life? (P)
- Is explicit content in a narrative more impactful than subtle content? (C)
- At what stages during the development of our story should we seek advice from authors? (S)
- At what stage should we collaborate to help each other with their stories?
- What makes an interesting story? (S)
- Where would the story be set? (C)
- Why do we undergo change? (C)
- Is change necessary to human society? (C)
- Which people possess greater ability to adapt to change? (C)
- How will diversity and individuality of stories be ensured? (P)
- What purpose does this project serve to the community and how can it in turn also change or affect people's lives? (P)
- Is change a necessity in life? (C)
- Can change be avoided, and what would this lack of change cause? (C)
- Who will feel the effects of specific changes the most? (C)
- Why is change commonly perceived as a negative yet positive aspect of life? (C)
- How often does change occur? (C)
- Why does change never change? (C)
- Can a writer's method of writing a story influence the reader's opinion of that change? (S)
- When and why is change feared or not wanted? (C)
- What emotions are associated with change? (C)
- When and why is change necessary? (C)
- What is the best time period in which to set a short story about change? (C)

LIFE STORY RESEARCH

USE THESE QUESTIONS TO INTERVIEW YOUR LOVED ONE ABOUT THEIR MOMENT OF CHANGE

1. IN WHAT COUNTRY WERE YOU BORN?

2. IN WHAT CITY, TOWN OR LOCATION DID YOU GROW UP?

3. WHAT WAS THE WEATHER, FOOD AND NEIGHBOURHOOD LIKE THERE?

4. WHAT WERE THE PEOPLE LIKE? (RELIGION, CUSTOMS, HOW RICH OR POOR, EDUCATION LEVEL, TYPES OF JOBS AVAILABLE, FASHION, POLITICS)

5. IN WHAT YEAR DID YOUR SIGNIFICANT MOMENT OF CHANGE HAPPEN? (1950S, 1980S, TODAY?)

6. DESCRIBE YOUR SIGNIFICANT MOMENT OF CHANGE (ENCOURAGE THEM TO GIVE SENSORY DETAILS)

7. WHAT MAJOR HISTORICAL EVENTS WERE HAPPENING IN YOUR COUNTRY AT THAT TIME?

8. WHAT DID YOU LOOK LIKE AT THIS TIME OF CHANGE? (HAIR AND EYE COLOUR, CLOTHING STYLE, HEIGHT, ETC)

REPRODUCIBLE – PART TWO: SAMPLE PROJECTS YEAR 8 – 3. LIFE STORIES

LIFE STORIES MATRIX

CHAPTER AND PAGE NO.	NARRATIVE DEVICES characterisation, structure, voice, motif, symbols, visual elements, figurative language, dialogue, mood, theme, imagery	SIGNIFICANT MOMENTS OR EXPERIENCES	CHALLENGE POSED TO CHARACTER	LESSONS LEARNT

CREATE ♫

This stage of the project is all about crafting a quality short story. Try to spend time with each student working on their life story, which will be based on the information gathered from the interview with their loved one. This is an individual writing task; however, students should work in writing teams – where the students actively seek and give feedback on their narratives as they plan, draft and edit.

PLANNING THE LIFE STORY

We've found that getting students to graphically represent their plot is an effective way to plan. Encourage them to create a plot diagram on A3 or butcher's paper that is clearly labelled, indicating elements such as the orientation, backfill, rising action, complication, resolution and coda (if applicable). If you have students who wish to subvert the traditional narrative structure, that's great, but it's still recommended that they plan in a traditional way first, and then move the elements around later. On another piece of paper, have students create character portraits for the main character(s). They should give as much detail as possible – remind them that not all this detail will be directly referenced in the story, but knowing a lot about a character will make for a stronger narrative. Remind students to use their completed Life Stories Research sheets to support this step. Breaking down the planning process in this way will (hopefully) result in a better product at the end.

BEGINNING TO WRITE

Using this information, it is now time for students to write the first draft of the story. This stage is enhanced by sharing with students quotes about the writing process from famous writers, with a focus on how difficult the process can be, and the need for lots of trial and error. Students may feel more confident if they receive peer or teacher feedback after they write each paragraph.

NOTE: At some point during the Create stage of the project, you will want to run one or two lessons of explicit instruction relating to the mechanics of writing. Our experience is that students often need the greatest support with sentence structure (especially complex sentences that use a range of clause types), punctuating dialogue and using figurative language effectively to enhance descriptions. You know your students best, so it is that we leave it to you to decide how you will develop your students' skills in these areas.

FORMATIVE ASSESSMENT 2

some strategies you might like to use to check students' understanding and skills at this stage of the

de warm and cool feedback (such as "star, star, wish" or medals and missions) on students' ive plans.

one lesson should be devoted to peer assessment of the draft stories.

due date for completed drafts and give feedback on these using the Life Stories checklist.

LIFE STORY CHECKLIST

SHORT STORY GOALS	NEEDS MORE WORK	OKAY	GOOD
Does the writer use a variety of sentence types to engage the reader?			
Does the story have dramatic changes in situations – from happy to sad, etc.?			
Has the writer included at least one or two well-developed characters?			
Has the writer composed a story that makes the reader both laugh and cry?			
Has the writer included slang and language appropriate to the character's world?			
Has the writer included descriptive language to help the reader see the character and settings?			
Is dialogue used correctly to help the reader learn more about the character?			

MEDALS: (most effective aspects of this short story)

MISSIONS: (main aspects of this short story that need improvement)

SHARE

Once students have received peer feedback on their stories and they have been refined in light of suggestions, they will need to be submitted to you for final assessment. This is an essential step for two reasons. One, you need to assess the final product to see what your students have learnt and where weaknesses still exist. Two, these stories are to be published in a hard copy collection, and students need to receive as much feedback as possible to ensure they have produced a quality story, worthy of publication.

Ensure you leave enough time between the completion of the stories and the book launch to have the stories printed using an online service like Blurb – they have an eBook option as well, which makes a great present for grandparents. Any other options for publishing are fine. Try to seek funding support from the school executive or Parents and Citizens (P & C). Seeing their work printed in a "real" book is exciting and rewarding for students.

The second part of the Share stage is the book launch. Have students create the invitations, book the space and organise the setting up of the venue, including bringing refreshments on the day. Have some students volunteer to read favourite excerpts from their story and to get feedback from the audience (or a panel of experts) on what they enjoyed. Copies of the books can be given to the loved one, and other copies sold with the proceeds going to a literacy-related charity such as the Indigenous Literacy Foundation.

FORMATIVE ASSESSMENT 3

Below are some strategies you might like to use to check students' understanding and skills at this stage of the project.

- Assess the final story using a modification of the checklist used for the drafts
- Assess students' creative-thinking skills using the BIE rubric (found at the back of this book)
- Have students do practice presentations and readings of story excerpts

YEAR 8

4. SOULE OF THE AGE

PROJECT AT A GLANCE:

 **DRIVING QUESTION:** Why do we continue to value the life and works of William Shakespeare?

 DISCOVER: Students will discover the biography of William Shakespeare; the social, cultural and political context of the Elizabethan world; and engage with a range of Shakespeare's works.

 CREATE: Students will work in small teams to curate information about a specific aspect of Shakespeare's life and/or works, and then create an engaging and interactive display.

 SHARE: Students' displays will be part of the Soule of the Age Shakespeare Fair for their school's student body.

 ASSESSMENT: Presentation on Shakespeare's life and times; team display

 21ST-CENTURY SKILLS: ICT, collaboration, research skills, creative thinking, time management, organisation and communication

LITERACY: *grammar* – clause types, verbs, adjectives, adverbs, sentence types; *reading* – questioning, making connections, visualising, monitoring; *punctuation* – commas, apostrophes, dashes

TYPE OF TEXT: persuasive (display for festival) and imaginative (plays/sonnets)

LANGUAGE FEATURES OF TEXTS: iambic pentameter, blank verse, soliloquy, aside, embedded stage directions, apostrophe, allusions, imagery, figurative language, symbolism, paradox

TEXTS: A range of Shakespeare plays and sonnets: *Shakespeare's Restless World* by Neil MacGregor (both the book [2014] and BBC World podcasts); *Shakespeare in Love* (Dir. John Madden, 1999); *Tales from Shakespeare* by Charles and Mary Lamb (1807); *YOLO Juliet* by Brett Wright (2015); and *A Midsummer Night #nofilter* by Brett Wright (2016).

Why do we continue to value the life and works of William Shakespeare?

Discover:
- The life and times of William Shakespeare
- A range of Shakespeare's literary works, including extracts from his plays

Assessment:

Create:
- Content about a specific aspect of Shakespeare's life and times and/or literary works in order to design an engaging and interactive display that answers the driving question

Assessment:

Share:
- Your expert knowledge of Shakespeare with the student body at your school as part of the inaugural Soule of the Age Shakespeare Fair

Assessment:

BEFORE YOU BEGIN

CONTACT EXPERTS

There are a number of experts that you can get involved in this project. The point at which they are involved will be determined by the expert that you choose. Some possible experts include: a director or actors from a local theatre company; an academic specialising in Shakespeare; or a curator from a local museum or art gallery.

PLAN THE HOOK LESSON

As always, there is a range of options for how to launch your project to engage your students' interests. You could focus on any element of the project, including the themes of Shakespeare's plays, aspects of Shakespeare's life or language, Elizabethan or medieval history, the theatre, or curation.

DISCOVER

The first part of every project should be handing out the project outline and establishing what students feel they need to know to successfully complete the project. To help you understand the types of questions that students could be asking at the Need to Know stage, look at the questions generated by our Year 8 students when they began this same project (on the following page). Don't give this copy to your class, rather use it as a teacher resource to help you guide your students to similar types of inquiry questions.

This project has an extended inquiry phase because students must engage with the biography of William Shakespeare; the social, cultural and political context of the Elizabethan world; and the work of Shakespeare. Of course, how you decide to get your students to engage with the texts is up to you and highly dependent on the students themselves. Some teachers will want their students to engage with Shakespeare's distinctive style through a whole-class close reading of an entire play. Some teachers will read extracts of a few plays, as well as have students watch scenes from film adaptations. Other teachers may have their students engage with the story of the plays and watch YouTube videos that explain key aspects. Engaging with Shakespeare's sonnets is also a useful activity. Ultimately, students are required to discover what makes Shakespeare's writing continue to resonate with people – this might be through his plots, characters, themes and distinctive writing style – through a process of guided or independent inquiry. A research task handout has been included with this unit to help guide your students' inquiry into the life of Shakespeare.

Following the initial independent, guided and collaborative research into the life and works of Shakespeare, students must then negotiate with you and the class on what specific aspect of his life and times they would like to explore more deeply with their team. This will be the basis of their exhibition, and once this is decided they will progress to the Create stage of the project.

FORMATIVE ASSESSMENT 1

Below are some strategies you might like to use to check students' understanding and skills at this stage of the project.

- Quiz students on their knowledge of the play/plays/poems set for study
- Check students' understanding of the project through individual interviews
- Students could write a report on Shakespeare's life
- Have students write analytical paragraphs on one of the texts studied
- Students could write a half-page response to the driving question under exam-style conditions

KWL TABLE

Use a KWL table like the one below to work out what you already *know* that will help you to succeed at each stage of the project, what you want to *learn* and *how* you think you can learn what you need to in order to succeed.

WHAT WE KNOW ...	WHAT WE WANT TO LEARN ...	HOW WE AIM TO LEARN IT ...

REPRODUCIBLE – PART TWO: SAMPLE PROJECTS YEAR 8 – 4. SOULE OF THE AGE

SHAKESPEARE RESEARCH TASK

Our PBL focus question makes the assumption that our class knows who William Shakespeare was. But this simply isn't true! All we know, as a class, is that he was "an old guy who spoke funny". This knowledge just isn't going to be enough to help us solve our perplexing problem — just why do people continue to value the literary works of Shakespeare?

We need to ask ourselves the following question:

Who was William Shakespeare?

To answer this question, you are going to have to do some research. You will complete this research in your PBL teams over two lessons in class. Your sources of information will be both print (books) and electronic (the internet) — but make sure that you record your sources of information and only use them as inspiration for your writing: never cut and paste. You also have access to a teacher — we are very handy, use us wisely.

In your groups, you need to find information about:

- William Shakespeare's life
- William Shakespeare's world
- William Shakespeare's theatre.

This information needs to be presented in an engaging format — your audience is your classmates. How will you make this information interesting and fun for them?

Some online tools you might like to use to make your presentation more interesting include:
- Xtranormal
- Glogster
- Pixton comics
- Prezi
- SlideShare

Let's see who can make discovering Shakespeare the most interesting!

SOULE OF THE AGE – NEED TO KNOW QUESTIONS

- What universal themes and concepts has Shakespeare explored in his texts?
- How do the themes that are explored in the text relate to Shakespeare's context?
- How does Shakespeare use tragedy to explore the themes and context relevant to his context?
- How has Shakespeare managed to use such transcending themes in his texts, leading them to remain relevant to this day?
- When did Shakespeare live?
- Is there a common theme that Shakespeare favours?
- How does Shakespeare use humour to display relevant themes and concepts?
- Why does Shakespeare use paradoxes to explore concepts?
- Why do we still study the themes and concepts present in Shakespeare's plays?
- Do concepts used go across different Shakespeare texts?
- What is the least common theme Shakespeare utilises?
- Are any concepts present in Shakespeare's tragedies still present in modern day society's texts and ideas?
- Were the themes and concepts used within Shakespearean plays controversial during his time?
- If Shakespeare was alive today, what would be an overarching theme he would choose to address in his works?
- Was Shakespeare more effective at portraying contemporary concepts and universal themes through his tragedies or his comedies?
- What is the worst theme he used?
- What ideas are shown in Shakespeare's texts?
- What theme/concepts recur throughout Shakespeare's writing?
- What symbols did Shakespeare intentionally/unintentionally avoid in his texts and why?
- What is the theme in most of Shakespeare's comedies?
- How do themes from Shakespeare's times translate to modern times?
- Why are these specific themes used?
- Why is tragedy a common theme?
- What are the repetitive elements of the contextual depth of Shakespeare's works?
- Did Shakespeare have any children?
- Why is the theme/concept of Shakespearean comedy so different to comedy today?
- How did Shakespeare integrate themes into his plays?
- Are Shakespeare's plays ever funny, or are they always sad?
- Are there any recurring stylistic features throughout Shakespeare's works?
- Are there any stories that have more than one theme?
- How have the concepts portrayed in his works influenced modern literature?
- Does Shakespeare use frequent themes of morbidity due to personal experiences?
- How did Shakespeare incorporate and manipulate a wide range of themes and concepts for such a diverse audience?
- How heavily are Shakespeare's past experiences reflected in his themes, plot, etc.?
- How does Shakespeare use ethnic characters to incorporate themes?
- Are any concepts in Shakespeare's plays inspired by something he disliked about society?
- How closely linked are his characters and themes and his life experiences?
- Why and how do we relate to Shakespeare's characters?
- Did Shakespeare base some of the concepts of his plays on his own personal experiences?

SHAKESPEARE'S IMAGERY

Shakespeare's plays are dense with imagery. He has many of his main characters speak with beautifully poetic voices. Some poetic devices that you may have noticed as you read through his sonnets or extracts of his plays include metaphor, simile, personification, hyperbole, onomatopoeia and alliteration. These techniques are used to create mood and imagery.

See if you can find examples of the following type of imagery as you engage with some of Shakespeare's works:

TACTILE IMAGERY
Example: _____

OLFACTORY IMAGERY
Example: _____

AURAL IMAGERY
Example: _____

VISUAL IMAGERY
Example: _____

CELESTIAL IMAGERY
Example: _____

RELIGIOUS IMAGERY
Example: _____

DISEASE IMAGERY
Example: _____

DEATH IMAGERY
Example: _____

BLOOD IMAGERY
Example: _____

SUPERNATURAL IMAGERY
Example: _____

NATURAL IMAGERY
Example: _____

NIGHT AND DAY IMAGERY
Example: _____

ANIMAL IMAGERY
Example: _____

CREATE 🎵

During the Create stage of this project, students will be working in small teams to design an interactive and engaging display that answers the driving question with a specific focus on a chosen aspect of Shakespeare's life and times. Speak with students about the parameters for their exhibition, such as the physical space that each team will have, the age of the attendees, the amount of time the attendees have to engage with the exhibition and so on. Their display is part of a large fair, so they should think big and ensure they include interactive elements for their teenage audience.

When it comes to developing ideas for a display, students should be encouraged to engage with the Creative Thinking rubric (see the back of this book) to help them appreciate what it means to be a creative thinker. Special focus should be drawn to the benefit of ideation – generating a wide range of possible inclusions in the exhibition before selecting the best ideas by carefully and objectively considering the pros and cons of each. Remind students that the best idea is one to which all team members have contributed. Once teams have decided on their best idea for their exhibition, they should create a rough visualisation using butcher's paper or a whiteboard, and then seek teacher feedback to make sure they're on the right track.

Below are a list of possible aspects of Shakespeare's life and times that students might wish to focus on:

- Shakespeare's childhood life in Stratford-upon-Avon
- Shakespeare's comedies
- Shakespeare's tragedies
- Shakespeare's histories
- Shakespeare's sonnets
- Witchcraft in Elizabethan times
- Shakespeare's insults
- Shakespeare's villains
- Shakespeare's heroes and heroines
- Elizabethan clothing and weapons
- The Globe Theatre
- Elizabethan food and drink
- Elizabethan entertainment, e.g. bear baiting.

FORMATIVE ASSESSMENT 2

This project is driven by quality teamwork. Give students the opportunity to comment on their collaborative skills (and to focus them on their role in the group) by giving them a mini reflection task like the one below. Our students completed this activity at the end of each lesson.

Three things I did this lesson to help develop my team's Shakespeare fair display are:

1.

2.

3.

4.

Signed: (all team members and teacher)

SHARE

The final presentation for this project is a very big event — a medieval fair for students' school peers. Help teams plan their time wisely, and make sure that each team member has a clear understanding of their individual roles and responsibilities. We find that having students use the Project Management Log helps with time management and organisation, as well as with collaboration. Students should use each lesson to guide their work. A blank copy of the Project Management Log can be found in the Additional Resources section at the back of this book. To keep the momentum up with students, have them create promotional material for the event, such as posters to put up around the school, articles in the school newsletter, posts on the school's social media platforms and announcements at assembly.

Remember that this stage of a project, especially one with a large-scale Share stage, can be stressful. Avoid rushing students or being overly critical. It is important that students know that the learning comes through the process, and the celebration comes from the learning. Most importantly, make sure that this stage of the project is fun.

YEAR 8

5. STEAMPUNK STORIES

PROJECT AT A GLANCE:

 **DRIVING QUESTION:** What does the future hold for humanity?

 DISCOVER: Students will research artificial intelligence, automation and dystopia as well as the language forms and features of steampunk fiction. Students will also learn to write short imaginative, persuasive and informative texts.

 CREATE: Students will individually compose a short, steampunk-inspired imaginative, persuasive or informative text answering the driving question.

 SHARE: The class will publish students' compositions in a zine called *Steampunk Stories*.

Take it further: Have students create their zine for a specific audience such as the residents at a local retirement village or nursing home, a preschool, or a primary school.

 ASSESSMENT: Students will be assessed on their short text — the plan, draft and final product.

 21ST-CENTURY SKILLS: critical thinking, ethical understanding, research skills, creative thinking

LITERACY: *grammar* – pronouns, verbs, compound words, sentence types, conjunctions, grammatical theme; *reading* – visualising, questioning, making connections; *punctuation* – commas, quotation marks, hyphens, parentheses

TYPE OF TEXT: informative, imaginative and persuasive

LANGUAGE FEATURES OF TEXTS: Dependent on type of text selected by student.

TEXTS: *It's Alive!: Artificial Intelligence from the Logic Piano to Killer Robots* by Toby Walsh (2017); *Machinarium* game http://machinarium.net/; *The Golden Compass* (Dir. Chris Weitz, 2007); *Howl's Moving Castle* (Dir. Hayao Miyazaki, 2004); *Steampunk! An Anthology of Fantastically Rich and Strange Stories* (Kelly Link and Gavin Grant, 2011); *Year Million* – National Geographic (2017)

What does the future hold for humanity?

Research and Imagine:

- Research the impact that automation and artificial intelligence may have on the future
- Research how people have represented their visions of the future through steampunk art and literature
- Imagine what the future might hold for humanity and our home planet

Assessment

Compose and Contribute:

- Compose an imaginative, informative or persuasive text that conveys a vision of the future for humanity
- Contribute your composition to a zine called Steampunk Stories

Assessment

Publish and Share:

- Publish your zine and share it with the general public through your local library and bookshops
- Add a link to a digital edition of the zine in your school newsletter

Assessment

REPRODUCIBLE – PART TWO: SAMPLE PROJECTS YEAR 8 – 5. STEAMPUNK STORIES

BEFORE YOU BEGIN

CONTACT EXPERTS

For this project, you may wish to involve content or form experts. The content of this project is related to artificial intelligence, automation and the impact they will have on the future of humanity. In relation to this aspect of the project you may wish to involve ex-students currently studying robotics or philosophy at university, an academic or expert in artificial intelligence and automation, or even a futurist. Another element is the short story form of the texts being studied. You may wish to involve an academic who is either specialising in short stories, or is well acquainted with the steampunk genre.

PLAN THE HOOK LESSON

For this project, a hook lesson involving play is essential. The style of steampunk is often playful, despite the more serious themes. Some possible hook lesson activities include:

- playing the first level of *Machinarium*
- dressing up in steampunk-style outfits and taking photos in a "photo booth"
- turn the classroom into a craft space and have students create visual representations of the future
- set up the classroom like a cinema and watch the film *Hugo* (Dir. Martin Scorsese, 2011) or *The Golden Compass* with popcorn and lolly bags.

DISCOVER

This stage of the project will include teacher-directed and student-directed learning. Looking at the project outline, it is clear that there are three main elements to the inquiry for this project. How much support and direction you give students in their inquiry is dependent on the skill level of your students. Here is a quick overview of the three elements that students will need to discover at this stage of the project.

1. *Research the impact that automation and artificial intelligence may have on the future.* To do this you might invite a guest speaker to present on these issues and answer students' questions. You might provide students with a range of digital texts and books from the library for them to use for independent research. You might watch the documentary series *Year Million* by National Geographic (2017), or you might have students read extracts of the article "The AI Revolution" by Toby Walsh (2017), available at *goo.gl/14zaUg*.

2. *Research how people have represented their visions of the future through steampunk art and literature.* This is your opportunity to provide students with access to a range of texts – be sure to include imaginative and persuasive texts for students to analyse. You may wish to run this part of the Discover stage as direct instruction with a deep focus on one extended text, such as a novel or a film, or you might wish to run it as teacher-guided inquiry where students are given a scaffold for their response to the texts. An activity sheet based on the online game *Machinarium* has been included on the following pages – this is an activity to help students develop their descriptive writing. It is also a lot of fun playing the game.

3. *Imagine what the future might hold for humanity and our home planet.* This element requires students to feel very safe in their imaginings, and works well following engagement with a range of steampunk genre texts. Encourage students to use the creative thinking rubric (in the back of this book) to help push themselves to move beyond their first idea, and beyond replication of existing ideas. This vision will likely be the basis of your students' imaginative, informative or persuasive composition for the zine.

FORMATIVE ASSESSMENT 1

- Hold a class debate on the benefits of artificial intelligence to humanity.
- Have students write answers to their identified Need to Know questions.
- Give students a quiz on the features of informative, imaginative and persuasive texts.
- Have students write a mini essay or report on the ideas, structure and language features of the steampunk genre.

PART TWO: SAMPLE PROJECTS YEAR 8 – 5. STEAMPUNK STORIES

MACHINARIUM

Using an online game to inspire steampunk-style descriptive writing

http://machinarium.net/demo/

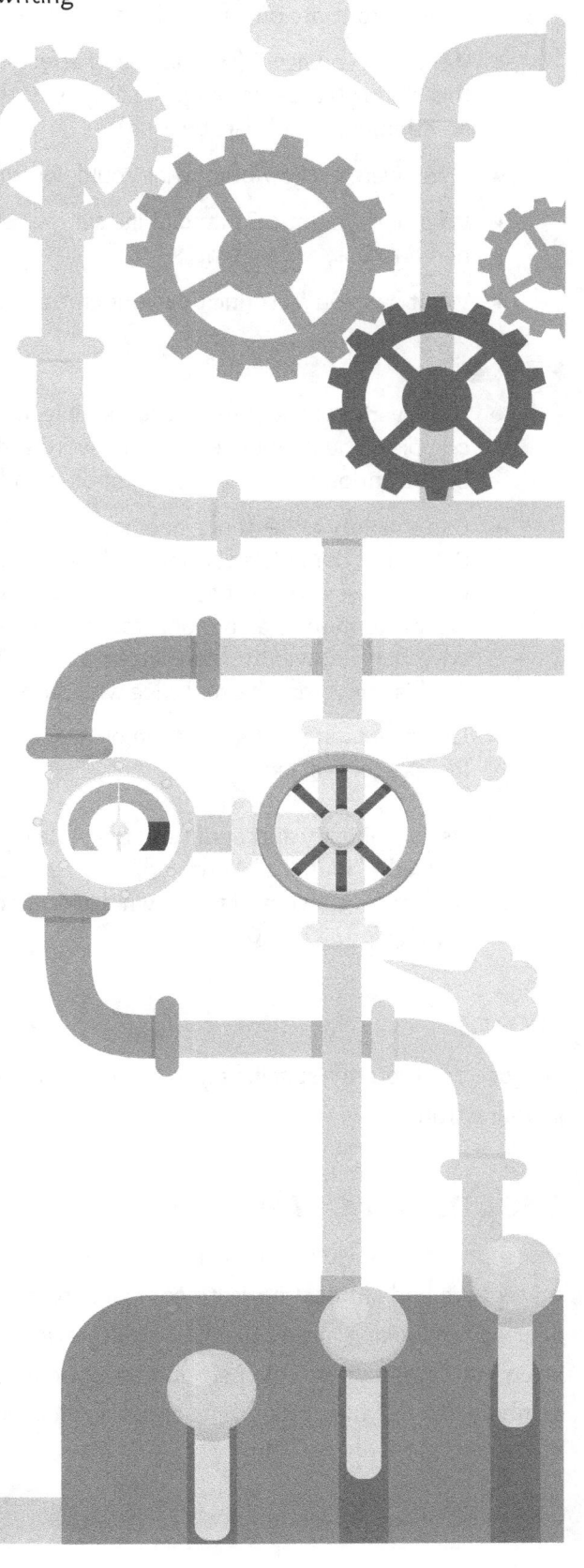

TASK 1

1. Watch the opening to the game Machinarium and complete levels one, two and three. Then Complete a character profile for the robot.

TIP:

Be as original as you can – look at the style of the art, look deep into the background landscape/setting, look closely at the robot …

- Who is he/she? Give him/her a name.
- Where is he/she from?
- What's his/her background?
- Where is he/she going?
- Why?
- Who are his/her friends?
- Who is his/her family?
- Who are his/her enemies?

TASK 2

2. Select one of the game levels or a cut scene (the little bits of animation you can't control between levels) and write a description of it. You may only write about one part of a level/scene. Try to get your reader to *imagine* the setting, characters and action; to *feel* emotions for the characters, setting and action; and to *think* about the characters, setting and action.

PROFESSIONAL WRITING TIPS

Imagine you are looking at this scene from within the world itself. Write a detailed description of the scene.

CONTENT

Focus on the FIVE senses:

- What can you *see*? (i.e. in the landscape, but also include descriptions of the characters and what is right in front of you, in the sky, at your feet, etc.)
- What can you *hear*? (i.e. the sound effects of the game, but also what would you hear as a character in this world? Metal scraping, the engine of the flying machine, the dialogue of the characters, your own breathing or your heart beating)
- If you were in the world, what could you *smell*?
- What can you *taste*? (*literally* like saliva, last night's garlic pizza, oily air and *figuratively* like fear, nervousness, excitement)
- What can you *feel*? (include your emotions)

STYLE

- Use a variety of sentence types: simple, compound and complex. You might even use one-word sentences to draw our attention to an object, action or sound.
- Use a variety of sentence beginnings (grammatical theme). Draw your reader's attention to different aspects of the scene by being clever with the beginning of your sentences. If you want to draw attention to an action, start the sentence with a verb or an adverb. If you want to draw attention to a feature of a character, like his feet, start the sentence with a noun or an adjective.
- Use interesting verbs. For example, use the word "shuffled" instead of "walked".
- Use vocabulary appropriate to the style of writing. This is steampunk, so use words like "hissed", "metallic", "guzzled", "screeched", "hummed", "robotic" and "cogs". Steampunk writers have invented their own words; find some here: *http://brassgoggles.co.uk/forum/index.php?topic=13753.0*.

GENRE

Because this is quite a specific style of game — steampunk — you should try to use elements of this style in your writing.

DESCRIPTIVE LANGUAGE

You should try to use poetic techniques to help your reader experience what is being described. Use **metaphors** and **similes** to create comparisons and images; use **personification** to give your reader a new way of looking at an object; use **alliteration** and **assonance** to create a musical effect and draw attention to certain words; use **onomatopoeia** to capture sounds of objects and people; and use **symbols** to help your reader think about an idea, person or place more carefully.

REPRODUCIBLE – PART TWO: SAMPLE PROJECTS YEAR 8 – 5. STEAMPUNK STORIES

CREATE 🎵

There are many collaborative learning and critical thinking strategies you can use to get students to develop their ideas about steampunk, short stories and the driving question. You may wish to use some of these: think/pair/share, star-bursting, hexagonal thinking, lotus diagrams, hot potato, jigsaws or Venn diagrams.

Students will work in critical friend teams to plan, draft and edit their individual short steampunk compositions. Encourage students to read each other's plans and drafts and to give constructive feedback using the "praise, inform, praise" or "star, star, wish" feedback method. This will allow students to give both positive and constructive feedback. To develop peer-assessment skills, have the class co-construct a set of criteria, or a checklist, for a high-quality steampunk-inspired imaginative, persuasive and informative composition. Model to the class how to use these criteria to give peer feedback, with a focus on identifying where specific criterion have or have not been addressed. Students should be encouraged to give medals and missions for the composition using the language of the criteria. For more information on this process, read the "A Word on PBL and Assessment" section at the beginning of this book.

FORMATIVE ASSESSMENT 2

Below are some strategies you might like to use to check students' understanding and skills at this stage of the project.

- Use different checklists for each type of text. The best way to do this is to spend a lesson with students grouped by their chosen type of texts, creating their own checklist for peer and self-assessment. A blank checklist proforma has been included in the "Part Three: Additional Resources" section.
- Check student learning journals to assess progress and understanding.

SHARE 👥

This is quite an academic and intellectually challenging project. The concepts are complex and the steampunk genre will be entirely new for most students. For some students, just getting their short text written will be cause for celebration. To show how you value the challenge your students have undergone and the work that they have produced, organise for their compositions to be collected into the *Steampunk Stories* zine. A zine can be both hard copy and digital.

To further celebrate your students' achievements, you might like to invite your guest expert back to hear readings from selected compositions. Organise one or two students to speak about the project – reflecting on what they enjoyed and what they found challenging. Friends and family could be invited as well, and they will certainly be impressed by what your students have learnt during this project.

FORMATIVE ASSESSMENT 3

The final personal essays can be assessed using a modified version of the co-constructed criteria or checklists used during the Create stage of this project. Reflection is an essential part of the project process, so you might like students to take some time to answer the following eight questions:

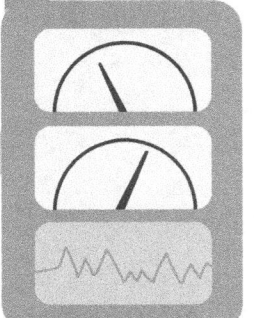

1. One of the learning goals of this project was to be able to write a steampunk-inspired composition that answers the driving question. How well did you achieve this goal?

2. During this project, you engaged with some complex ideas about the future. Which ideas did you find the most challenging? Why?

3. What writing skills did you develop as a result of creating a short composition for the zine?

4. What is something that was hard for you at the start of the project, but is easy now?

5. This project aimed to develop your appreciation for how the steampunk genre conveys ideas about the future. Discuss how this project allowed you to do so.

6. What in our class has made the biggest impact on your learning during this project? Why?

7. What is something the teacher could have done to make this project better?

8. If you could turn back time and do this project again, what would you do differently?

PART THREE
ADDITIONAL RESOURCES

A range of additional resources has been included to support you as you work through your first projects in English and then beyond as you begin designing your own projects. These additional resources include:

- **The project design grid (p. 144).** This grid will help you decide on the hook lesson, product, audience and guest expert. When you become more confident with PBL, you may also like to give this to your students to design their own projects.

- **Practice projects (pp. 145–146).** Use these outlines for single-lesson micro projects when introducing the structure of PBL to your students.

- **Formative assessment strategies list (p. 147).** This brief list gives you an overview of some of the key formative assessment strategies that we use to help us track student learning throughout projects. Google is your friend with this resource – for each strategy you will find numerous resources online.

- **Blank checklist (p. 148).** We love a checklist! They're great for peer and self-assessment. You or your students can modify this checklist.

- **Blank KWHL table (p. 149).** We use a KWL or KWHL table at the beginning of each project – it's perfect for pre-testing prior knowledge, as well as for generating the important Need to Know questions that will drive students' learning.

- **Blank project calendar (p. 150).** Use this in the early stages of a project to help students visualise their learning trajectory, and to help keep them on track.

- **Project outline proforma (p. 151).** This document is essentially a blank slate for designing your own project. It gives you a sense of the key elements that should be included – the driving question plus the content and learning experiences relevant to each stage of learning (Discover, Create, Share). Space has also been given to indicate formative assessment and due dates where applicable.

- **Project team contract (p. 152).** Have students complete this at the beginning of a project, and refer to it if there are issues with group cohesion, or a student is not working effectively.

- **Project management log (p. 153).** This handy sheet helps students with their time management, organisation and collaboration.

- **Project essentials checklist (p. 154).** This is for you to use to evaluate the projects you run with your students. Running through this handy list will help you to ensure that your students are participating in PBL, and not just "doing a project". Use this for EVERY project.

- **Rubrics (pp. 155–159).** Throughout the sample projects in this book, we have made reference to the use of assessment rubrics for helping students develop essential 21st-century skills such as collaboration, digital citizenship, and critical and creative thinking. A number of these have been included here to support your students' development of the skills.

PROJECT DESIGN GRID

HOOK	EXPERT	PRODUCT	AUDIENCE
Model building	Academic	Video (vlog/paper slide/Minecraft screencast)	Principal/HT/teachers
Watching YouTube	Author	Documentary	Class within school
Drama activities	Director (film/theatre)	Film	Class in another school (face to face or online via Skype)
Taking students outside	Celebrity	Website (Weebly, Wix)	Whole school
Garden health assessment and revamp	Engineer	Picture book	Grandparents
Tasting foods	Journalist	Novel/Novella	Local politician
Classroom cinema	Game designer	Book/eBook/iBook	Nursing home
Guest expert talk	Artist/Musician	Graphic novel	Preschool
Six-word story/memoir/play	Business person	Exhibition	Online
Twitter Q&A with expert	Community clubs/Organisations	Food stall	Local/State library
Art – painting	Chef/Baker	Innovative design and prototype	Local art gallery
Celebrity heads/Match the pictures	Fashion designer	Video game design	University campus
Introductory video from expert	Politician	Poetry performance/Reading	Youth workers
Skype call with expert	Sportsperson	*Horrible Histories* episode	Expert
Playing video games	Gardener	Interpretive dance	Parents and friends
Scavenger hunt	Non-government organisation (NGO) representative	Stage performance	Charity representatives

PRACTICE PROJECT 1

HOW CAN WE BUILD A STRONG ONE-METRE BRIDGE FROM SIMPLE MATERIALS?

DISCOVER:

- the best method of constructing a one metre bridge using the simple materials you are given by the teacher
- Materials:
- two A3 pieces of paper
- three lengths of sticky tape
- five paperclips
- one blob of blue tack.

CREATE:

- a one-metre-long bridge that is suspended between two classroom desks. Your bridge must be able to hold the weight of these objects:
- lead pencil (1 point)
- whiteboard marker (2 points)
- pair of scissors (4 points)
- calculator (4 points)
- stapler (6 points).

SHARE:

- your construction with the class and have its strength tested
- a photograph of your construction with an audience of teachers via Twitter - the most attractive design voted by Twitter will receive five bonus points.

REPRODUCIBLE – ADDITIONAL RESOURCES

PRACTICE PROJECT 2

You're living in a village that is constantly being attacked by dragons. The attacks are so frequent and swift that your village's resources are being significantly depleted. The king and queen of your village have asked interested people to submit a proposal and prototype for a dragon trap design that will save the village.

WHAT'S THE BEST DESIGN FOR A DRAGON TRAP?

DISCOVER:
- the strengths and weakness of dragons
- the best design for a successful dragon trap.

ASSESSMENT: Critical Thinking Collaboration

CREATE:
- a prototype for a successful dragon trap, using ONLY the materials given to you.

ASSESSMENT: Creativity and Innovation Collaboration

SHARE:
- your prototype with the king and queen and explain its design.

ASSESSMENT: Presentation

FAR-OUT AND FANTASTIC
FORMATIVE ASSESSMENT STRATEGIES

- GOALS/MEDALS/MISSIONS – DAILY, WEEKLY OR USING A CHECKLIST FOR A DRAFT
- HEXAGONAL THINKING
- QUIZZES
- TRAFFIC LIGHTS
- STAR-BURSTING
- THIRTY-SECOND CHECK-IN
- EXIT SLIPS
- SOLO TAXONOMY
- PUNK LEARNER RUBRIC
- RUBRICS FOR 21ST-CENTURY SKILLS
- BLOGGING
- KWHL TABLE
- TIMED WRITING CHALLENGES
- RUBRICS FOR PRODUCTS
- GALLERY WALK
- STAR, STAR, WISH
- THINK/PUZZLE/EXPLORE

REPRODUCIBLE – ADDITIONAL RESOURCES

NAME:						
CRITERIA		PEER ASSESSMENT #1			PEER ASSESSMENT #2		
		STILL LEARNING	ACHIEVED	ABOVE & BEYOND	DIDN'T	TRIED	DID
1							
2							
3							
4							
5							
6							
7							
8							
9							
10							

Medals: (main strengths of this _____)

Missions: (improvements needed for this _____)

REPRODUCIBLE – ADDITIONAL RESOURCES

KWHL TABLE

Use a KWHL table like the one below to work out what you already *know* that will help you to succeed at each element of the project, what you *want* to learn, *how* you think you can learn what you need to in order to succeed and what you have *learnt* through the project.

WHAT WE KNOW ...	WHAT WE WANT TO LEARN ...	HOW WE AIM TO LEARN IT ...	WHAT WE HAVE LEARNT ...

PROJECT CALENDAR

PROJECT:

DATES:

	MONDAY	TUESDAY	WEDNESDAY	THURSDAY	FRIDAY
PROJECT WEEK ONE					
PROJECT WEEK TWO					
PROJECT WEEK THREE					
PROJECT WEEK FOUR					

PART THREE - ADDITIONAL RESOURCES

PROJECT OUTLINE PERFORMA

DRIVING QUESTION:

SHARE:

CREATE:

DISCOVER:

ASSESSMENT:

ASSESSMENT:

ASSESSMENT:

 REPRODUCIBLE – ADDITIONAL RESOURCES

NOTE: As mentioned previously, one of the world's most reputable organisations in advocating quality Project Based Learning is the Buck Institute for Education. They share a wide range of very useful resources, and we are lucky enough to have been given permission to reproduce some of our favourites here for you in this book. The rubrics on the following pages and the "Project Essentials Checklist" are the creation of the hardworking and inspiring team at The Buck Institute for Education *(www.bie.org)*.

PROJECT TEAM CONTRACT	
PROJECT NAME	
TEAM MEMBERS	

OUR AGREEMENT

- We all promise to listen to each other's ideas with respect.
- We all promise to do our work as best as we can.
- We all promise to do out work on time.
- We all promise to ask for help if we need it.
- We all promise to _____

If someone on our team breaks one or more of our rules, the team may have a meeting and ask the person to follow our agreement. If the person still breaks the rules, we will ask our teacher to help find a solution.

DATE: _____

TEAM MEMBERS SIGNATURE:

_____   _____

_____   _____

_____   _____

_____   _____

REPRODUCIBLE – ADDITIONAL RESOURCES

PROJECT MANAGEMENT LOG: INDIVIDUAL GUIDE

DRIVING QUESTION:

NAME:

TASK	DATE DUE	STATUS	DONE

This document reproduced with permission from BIE

PROJECT ESSENTIALS CHECKLIST

DOES THE PROJECT ... ?	👍	👎	?
FOCUS ON SIGNIFICANT CONTENT AND AUTHENTIC ISSUES Students learn important subject matter content and address problems and issues from the world outside the classroom			
ORGANISE ACTIVITIES AROUND A DRIVING QUESTION OR CHALLENGE Students find the complex, open-ended question or challenge to be a meaningful focus for their work			
ESTABLISH A NEED TO KNOW AND DO Students are brought into the project by an entry event that captures interest and begins the inquiry process			
ENGAGE STUDENTS IN INQUIRY Students think deeply and ask further questions as they generate answers and solutions			
REQUIRE INNOVATION Students generate new answers and/or create unique products in response to the Driving Question or challenge			
DEVELOP 21ST-CENTURY SKILLS Students build critical and creative thinking, collaboration and presentation skills that are taught and assessed			
ENCOURAGE STUDENT VOICE AND CHOICE Students, with guidance from the teacher, make decisions that affect the course of the project			
INCORPORATE FEEDBACK AND REVISION Students use feedback to improve their work and create high-quality products			
CONCLUDE WITH A PUBLIC PRESENTATION Students exhibit products or present solutions, explain their work to others and respond to content- and process-focused questions			

REPRODUCIBLE – ADDITIONAL RESOURCES

CRITICAL THINKING RUBRIC FOR PBL

©2013 BUCK INSTITUTE FOR EDUCATION

CRITICAL THINKING OPPORTUNITY AT PHASES OF A PROJECT	BELOW STANDARD	APPROACHING STANDARD	AT STANDARD	ABOVE STANDARD ☐
LAUNCHING THE PROJECT: ANALYSE DRIVING QUESTION AND BEGIN INQUIRY	• I cannot explain what I would need to know to be able to answer the Driving Question • I still need to learn how another person might think differently about the Driving Question • I still need to learn how to ask questions about what our audience or product users might want or need	• I can identify a few things I would need to know to be able to answer the Driving Question • I can understand that another person might think differently about the Driving Question • I can ask a few questions about what our audience or product users might want or need	• I can explain what I would need to know to be able to answer the Driving Question • I can explain how different people might think about the Driving Question • I can ask lots of questions about what our audience or product users might want or need	
BUILDING KNOWLEDGE, UNDERSTANDING AND SKILLS: GATHER AND EVALUATE INFORMATION	• I still need to learn how to use information from different sources to help answer the Driving Question • I still need to learn how to think about whether my information is relevant or if I have enough	• I can use information from different sources to help answer the Driving Question, but I may have trouble putting it together • I can think about whether my information is relevant and if I have enough, but I don't always decide carefully	• I can use information from different sources to help answer the Driving Question • I can decide if my information is relevant and if I have enough	
DEVELOPING AND REVISING IDEAS AND PRODUCTS: USE EVIDENCE AND CRITERIA	• I still need to learn how to identify the reasons and evidence an author or speaker uses to support a point • I still need to learn how to decide if an idea for a product or an answer to the Driving Question is a good one • I still need to learn how to use feedback from other students and adults to improve my writing or my design for a product	• I can identify some of the reasons and evidence an author or speaker uses to support a point • I can tell when an idea for a product or an answer to the Driving Question is a good one, but cannot always say why • I can sometimes use feedback from other students and adults to improve my writing or my design for a product	• I can explain how an author or speaker uses reasons and evidence to support a point that helps me answer the Driving Question • I can explain how to decide if an idea for a product or an answer to the Driving Question is a good one • I can use feedback from other students and adults to improve my writing or my design for a product	
PRESENTING PRODUCTS AND ANSWERS TO DRIVING QUESTION: JUSTIFY CHOICES	• I still need to learn how to explain my ideas in an order that makes sense • I still need to learn how to use appropriate facts or relevant details to support my ideas	• I can explain my ideas, but some might be in the wrong order • I can use some facts and details to support my ideas, but they are not always appropriate and relevant	• I can explain my ideas in an order that makes sense • I can use appropriate facts and relevant details to support my ideas	

REPRODUCIBLE – ADDITIONAL RESOURCES

COLLABORATION RUBRIC FOR PBL: INDIVIDUAL PERFORMANCE

©2013 BUCK INSTITUTE FOR EDUCATION

	BELOW STANDARD	APPROACHING STANDARD	AT STANDARD	ABOVE STANDARD
TAKES RESPONSIBILITY	<ul><li>I need to prepare for and join team discussions</li><li>I need reminders to do project work</li><li>My project work is not done on time</li><li>I need to learn how to use feedback from others</li></ul>	<ul><li>I am usually prepared for and join team discussions</li><li>I do some project work, but sometimes need to be reminded</li><li>I complete most project work on time</li><li>I sometimes use feedback from others</li></ul>	<ul><li>I am prepared for work with the team; I have studied required material and use it to explore ideas in discussions</li><li>I do project work without having to be reminded</li><li>I complete project work on time</li><li>I use feedback from others to improve my work</li></ul>	☐
HELPS THE TEAM	<ul><li>I need to cooperate with my team and help the team solve problems</li><li>I need to learn how to help make discussions effective</li><li>I need to learn how to give useful feedback to others</li><li>I need to learn to offer to help others if they need it</li></ul>	<ul><li>I cooperate with the team but do not help it solve problems</li><li>I usually help make discussions effective, but do not always follow the rules, ask enough questions or express ideas clearly</li><li>I give feedback to others, but it may not always be helpful</li><li>I sometimes offer to help others if they need it</li></ul>	<ul><li>I help the team solve problems and manage conflicts</li><li>I help make discussions effective by following agreed-upon rules, asking and answering questions, clearly expressing ideas</li><li>I give helpful feedback to others</li><li>I offer to help others do their work if needed</li></ul>	
RESPECTS OTHERS	<ul><li>I am sometimes impolite or unkind to teammates (may interrupt, ignore others' ideas, hurt feelings)</li><li>I need to learn how to listen to other points of view and disagree kindly</li></ul>	<ul><li>I am usually polite and kind to teammates</li><li>I usually listen to other points of view and disagree kindly</li></ul>	<ul><li>I am polite and kind to teammates</li><li>I listen to other points of view and disagree kindly</li></ul>	

REPRODUCIBLE – ADDITIONAL RESOURCES

PRESENTATION RUBRIC FOR PBL

©2013 BUCK INSTITUTE FOR EDUCATION

	BELOW STANDARD	APPROACHING STANDARD	AT STANDARD	ABOVE STANDARD ☐
EXPLANATION OF IDEAS & INFORMATION	• Uses inappropriate facts and irrelevant details to support main ideas	• Chooses some facts and details that support main ideas, but there may not be enough, or some are irrelevant	• Chooses appropriate facts and relevant, descriptive details to support main ideas and themes	
ORGANISATION	• Does not include everything required in presentation • Presents ideas in an order that does not make sense • Does not plan timing of presentation well; it is too short or too long	• Includes almost everything required in presentation • Tries to present ideas in an order, but it doesn't always make sense • Presents for the right length of time, but some parts may be too short or too long	• Includes everything required in presentation • Presents ideas in an order that makes sense • Organises time well; no part of the presentation is rushed, too short or too long	
EYES & BODY	• Does not look at audience; reads notes • Fidgets or slouches a lot	• Makes some eye contact, but reads notes or slides most of the time • Fidgets or slouches a little	• Keeps eye contact with audience most of the time; only glances at notes or slides • Has a confident posture	
VOICE	• Speaks too quietly or not clearly • Does not speak appropriately for the situation (may be too informal or use slang)	• Speaks loudly and clearly most of the time • Speaks appropriately for the situation most of the time	• Speaks loudly and clearly • Speaks appropriately for the situation, using formal English when appropriate	
PRESENTATION AIDS	• Does not use audio/visual aids or media • Uses inappropriate or distracting audio/visual aids or media	• Uses audio/visual aids or media, but they sometimes distract from the presentation, or do not add to ideas and themes	• Uses well-produced audio/visual aids or media to add to main ideas and themes	
RESPONSE TO AUDIENCE QUESTIONS	• Does not answer audience questions	• Answers some audience questions, but not clearly or completely	• Answers audience questions clearly and completely	
PARTICIPATION IN TEAM PRESENTATIONS	• Not all team members participate; only one or two speak	• All team members participate, but not equally	• All team members participate for about the same length of time, and are able to answer questions	

REPRODUCIBLE – ADDITIONAL RESOURCES

CREATIVITY & INNOVATION RUBRIC FOR PBL

©2013 BUCK INSTITUTE FOR EDUCATION

PROCESS

CREATIVITY & INNOVATION OPPORTUNITY AT PHASES OF A PROJECT	BELOW STANDARD	APPROACHING STANDARD	AT STANDARD	ABOVE STANDARD ☐
LAUNCHING THE PROJECT — DEFINE THE CREATIVE CHALLENGE	• I may just "follow directions" without understanding why something needs to be created. • I still need to learn how to think about what people might need or like when they use or see what is created.	• I know that something needs to be created but cannot give detailed reasons why. • I have a basic idea of what people might need or like when they use or see what is created.	• I understand the reasons why something needs to be created. • I understand the needs and interests of the people who will use or see what is created.	
BUILDING KNOWLEDGE, UNDERSTANDING AND SKILLS — IDENTIFY SOURCES OF INFORMATION	• I use only the usual sources of information (website, book, article).	• I find one or two sources of information that are unusual.	• I find unusual ways to get information.	
DEVELOPING AND REVISING IDEAS AND PRODUCTS — GENERATE AND SELECT IDEAS	• I think of ideas for the product that are not new or original. • I pick an idea without deciding which one is best. • I still need to learn how to improve on the idea. • I still need to learn how to use feedback from others to improve written products.	• I think of some new ideas for the product. • I quickly decide which idea is best. • I might think about how to improve on the idea, but might not. • I use some feedback to make small changes in written products.	• I think of many new ideas for the product. • I carefully decide which idea is best. • I ask new questions and think about how to improve on the idea. • I use feedback from others to improve written products.	
PRESENTING PRODUCTS AND ANSWERS TO DRIVING QUESTION — PRESENT WORK TO USERS/TARGET AUDIENCE	• I present ideas and products in just the regular ways (show PowerPoint slides, read notes, have no audience involvement).	• I try to add some interesting touches to visual aids but they may not add much, or they may be distracting. • I try to involve the audience actively in the presentation but it is very quick or does not work well.	• I create visual aids that are interesting to see and hear. • I involve the audience actively in the presentation (ask them questions, have them do an activity).	

CREATIVITY & INNOVATION RUBRIC FOR PBL

©2013 BUCK INSTITUTE FOR EDUCATION

PROCESS

	BELOW STANDARD	APPROACHING STANDARD	AT STANDARD	ABOVE STANDARD
ORIGINALITY	• My product looks like things that have been seen before; it is not new or unique.	• My product has some new ideas, but it still looks mostly like things that have been seen before.	• My product is new, unique, surprising; shows a personal touch.	☐
VALUE	• My product is not useful or valuable by the people who use or see it. • My product would not work in the real world.	• My product is somewhat useful but it may not exactly meet the needs of people who use or see it. • My product might work in the real world, but might have problems.	• My product is seen as useful and valuable by the people who use or see it. • My product would work in the real world (not too hard, expensive, time-consuming to create).	
STYLE	• My product looks like other things like this; it is made in a traditional style. • My product has several pieces that do not fit together; it is a mishmash.	• My product has some interesting touches. • My product has some pieces that may be too much or do not fit together well.	• My product is well-made, impressive, designed with style. • My product's pieces all go well together.	

 REPRODUCIBLE — ADDITIONAL RESOURCES

ACKNOWLEDGEMENTS

I just wanted to take this opportunity to thank the amazing people in my life who supported me with writing this second PBL book:

Lee, Keenan and Balin – thank you for putting up with my writing-induced absent-mindedness, and for always being the reminder of why I do what I do.

Dad, Mum, K-J, Tammy and Ellicia – thank you for being the most loving, loyal, humble, generous and caring family a perfectionist, work-obsessed, scatterbrained little Jimmy could want.

Tina and Martin – thank you for your kindness, support and generosity. Oh, and for forgiving my poor housekeeping skills when I am hooked to my laptop writing!

Bimma, Ashleigh, Tanya and Kelli – thank you for being the best girl gang this spacey, anxious friend could ever ask for. Your incredible support, patience and empathy has helped me get through when I thought I could never get this book finished.

To the teachers – thanks for buying this book, and supporting Lee and me as we continue to commit ourselves to shaking up how young people are educated. Welcome to the revolution.

IMAGE CREDITS

www.freepik.com

p. 24, 38, 48–49, 64, 68, 80, 88, 97–98, 111, 136–142, 146 by Freepik

p. 30, 32–34, 44, 51–54, 95, 119–120, 122, 153 by Dooder

p. 43 by Balasoiu

p. 63: 'Microphones in reporter hands' by Makyzz

p. 88: 'Diary Vintage Banners' by macrovector

p. 102: 'Film Roll' by Starline

p. 110–112: 'ClipBoard' by iconicbestiary

p. 126, 133: 'Antique parchment' by Layerace

p. 136: 'Steampunk Character' by vvstudio

p. 145: 'Bridges icons collection' by Photoroyalty

www.freevector.com

p. 108: 'Halloween vector' by FreeVector

p. 126–133: 'William Shakespeare' by FreeVector

www.vecteezy.com

p. 47: 'The Hip Hop Man' by Vecteezy

www.istock.com

p38 by MicrovOne

www.ingramcontent.com/pod-product-compliance
Lightning Source LLC
Chambersburg PA
CBHW081917090526
44590CB00019B/3388